Flying High

The Life & Stories of
William L. Mikkelson

Copyright © 2019 by William L. Mikkelson

All Rights Reserved. No part of this book may be reproduced, stored in a retrieval system, or transmitted in any form or by any means, electronic, mechanical, photocopying, recording, or otherwise without the prior written permission of William L. Mikkelson and his assigns.

Flying High reflects the opinions, perceptions and memories of William L. Mikkelson. The stories they express within these pages are matters of personal opinion, not necessarily fact, and are in no way intended to be hurtful to any individual or group.

ISBN-13: 978-0-578-40152-2
Library of Congress Control Number: 2019914109

Crafted & Published by
Linda A. Hamilton
www.StoriestoLast.com
510-301-1997

Stories to Last

Flying High

The Life & Stories of
William L. Mikkelson

Acknowledgements

I dedicate this book to my dear wife of 68 years, Fern.

I would like to thank my wonderful children, grandchildren and great grandchildren for their love.

A special thank you to Wanda for encouraging me to tell my stories and for all her support. She has enriched my life and brought happiness to me.

I would like to acknowledge the skillful and artistic touch that Linda Parker Hamilton added to my life tales. And thank you to all my friends who are willing to read about little old me.

Table of Contents

Chapter One	Childhood	7
Chapter Two	Junior High at Central	61
Chapter Three	High School Years	75
Chapter Four	College Years	99
Chapter Five	Military Years	113
Chapter Six	Young Married Life	159
Chapter Seven	The Smoke-Craft Years	191
Chapter Eight	Semi-Retirement	247
Chapter Nine	Ski & Heliskiing Adventures	287
Chapter Ten	Looking Back	309

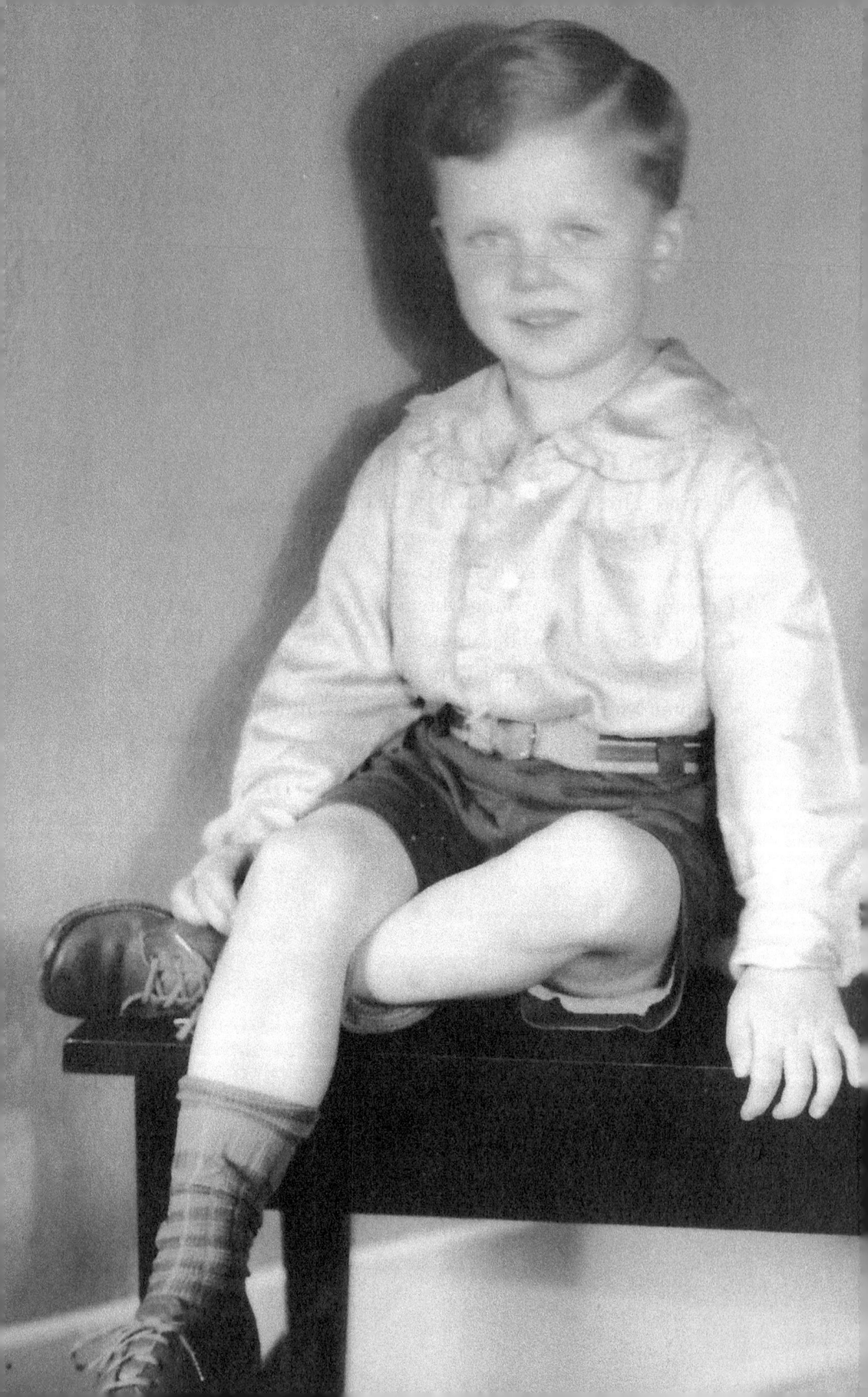

Chapter One

Childhood
1924 to 1936

RUMOR HAS IT, I FIRST MADE MYSELF KNOWN in this world right in the middle of my mother's birthday party on May 19, 1924. Of course, I have no memory of it! Coincidentally, my daughter Gail was later born close to my birthday on May 22, and a generation later, her son Eric was also born May 22, making this parent-child-birthday-pattern a Mikkelson tradition.

My life started in South St. Paul, Minnesota, where my father grew up and worked in his father's butcher shop, another Mikkelson tradition. When I came along, my mother was still a new mother to my brother Bob, who was born just eighteen months earlier (November 27, 1922). My parents, Alice and Harry, had been married in the Congregational Church in South St. Paul (June 10, 1921) and then moved to Milwaukee, Wisconsin, for a short time then back to St. Paul before Mother was ready to give birth to me, christened William Luther Mikkelson.

A Toddler on the Rails to Oregon

As a young family, we didn't stay in St. Paul long. In 1926, my father left ahead of my mother and my brother and me for Albany, Oregon, to secure a place for us to live and a job as a manager with the D. E. Nebergall Meat Company at the recommendation of my mom's brother, Dewey Greiner. Dewey had wanderlust, visiting various parts of the United States before settling into employment at a lumber mill in Oregon. There he fell in love with a local named Ivy Harkins, and Oregon became his lifelong home. He and Ivy married in 1924 and had two children, my cousins Jack and Shirlee.

Alice and her brother Earl, also known as Uncle Jack, 1920

Besides the promise of employment in a known field and independence from his father, it's likely that the opportunity to play baseball was also a draw for my dad to move to Oregon. There was an active semi-pro league in the northwest, and he loved baseball.

My mother, with us boys, just two and three-years old, lived temporarily with her parents in Minneapolis, just nine miles from St. Paul. One of my mother's other brothers, Earl (Jack or EJ) Greiner was teaching and playing semi-pro ball in North Dakota at the time. When Mom got the word from Dad that he was ready to receive us, she asked Uncle Jack, as we knew him, to accompany us to Oregon. Jack said yes and drove to Minneapolis in his Studebaker, picked up Alice, Bob and me and headed west via mom's hometown of Bottineau, then northwest to the Vantage District in Canada to visit family living there. Jack left the car in Saskatchewan where we caught the train to Albany, Oregon.

It was a long cross-country journey with two active toddlers. Of course, the train was the only option in 1926 since commercial flight wasn't yet in operation. This is significant to me since flying was such a huge part of my life as an adult.

In those days people dressed up to travel, women in hats and dresses, men in their suit coats and vests and matching trousers, pressed shirts and winter top coats. This is how my mother and Uncle Jack were adorned. In the years afterwards, my uncle liked to recount the story of holding me on his lap on the train when I guess I just had to go. "You peed all over my new suit!" he laughed whenever he told the story.

Jack ended up staying in Oregon, enrolling in Oregon State University and receiving his Bachelor of Science degree, after which he coached basketball and taught industrial art classes for ten years in Powers, Oregon, from 1928 to 1938. During that time, Jack married Eleanor Jane Miller of North Bend and they had two children, Dona and Earl. In 1938, they relocated to the larger community of McMinnville, home of Linfield College (founded in 1883) and fifty miles north of Albany, where Uncle Jack created a model high school industrial arts shop, and the family settled into a satisfying life.

> ***The Beginning of Commercial Flight***
>
> In 1924, only mail planes were operating commercially in the U.S. In 1926, the Air Commerce Act began to regularize commercial aviation by establishing standards, facilitation, and promotion and in 1927, Pan American Airlines was established. But passenger flight didn't really "take off" until after World War II).

Like my dad, he continued to play semi-pro baseball in the Oregon circuit. Jack eventually became mayor of the town because of his popularity and his intellect.

Settling into Albany

Nebergall Meat Company was a slaughterhouse and meat packing plant, one of many successful industrial plants in town producing varying goods. Albany, with a population of about 5,000 at that time, had become the manufacturing and transportation hub of the Willamette Valley as early as 1871 when Albany businessmen raised money to make sure the train came directly through the city. Prior to that, products and people traveled to and from Albany via coaches and steamboats. The town thrived with its seat at the confluence of the Calapooia and Willamette rivers and in the central valley, affording an overland thoroughfare from Sacramento to Portland and farther north to Seattle (It's no wonder Interstate 5 was eventually built in that south to north corridor). It was the Monteith brothers, entrepreneurs Walter and Thomas, who gave the town its name in 1847, honoring their hometown in New York. Over time, Albany became host to foundries, blacksmith shops, tanneries, furniture factories, carriage factories, a bag factory, a twine factory, flour and flax mills, creameries, farms, and sawmills. The logging industry had a major influence on the town throughout my life there. Flour, grain and produce were shipped regularly by river and rail to Portland and eastern cities.

Dad worked in the factory for a few years but resolved that he liked the retail side of the business more than the plant, so he next

Dad in the Pfeiffer's Market delivery truck circa 1930. It came in handy in the early years when we did not own a car.

worked as the manager in a butcher shop called Pfeiffer's Market, starting around 1929. Pfeiffer's Market shared a storefront with the Dooley Brothers grocery store and a hard goods store, with a dance studio on the second floor, located on Broadalbin between Second and Third Streets downtown.

The Pfeiffers were long-time residents of Albany. The first of them, Charles Pfeiffer built the Revere Hotel in downtown in 1877. Charles Jr. owned a men's clothing store. Franz Pfeiffer, a brother of Charles Jr., owned the market. An older guy by the time my dad worked for him, he had all the money he ever needed so never operated the shop, just owned it, leaving the day-to-day management to my dad, which suited them both.

After a half-dozen years of my daddy managing the shop as if it was his own, Mr. Pfeiffer sold the business to him, and it became Harry's Market sometime before 1936. Advertisements in the local newspaper in 1948 declared, "Harry's meat can't be beat!"

From very early on, the entire family, including my mother, spent a lot of time working in the butcher shop.

Growing Up in the Meat Business

Bob and I were put to work in the butcher shop when we were only six and seven years old. As Mikkelson boys, we had no choice. My only memories of the meat market involved working there, which I did into adulthood.

My first job as a little boy was cleaning the glass on the inside of the showcase on Sundays when the shop was closed. Then Bob and I would sweep the floors. The showcase, running underneath the length of the counter was an important aspect of the shop. It displayed all our goods. Customers would look through the glass at all the meats laid out on trays in rows, each marked with a price, five cents a chop or six cents a pound for hamburger, and make their decisions, often pointing to a specific cut of meat and giving their order to whoever was working behind the counter.

"Give me half a pound of hamburger and two pork chops, and please don't put that thick one in because I don't want to pay that much," one customer might say.

The showcase glass slanted in the front so no reflection would block the customers' view of the steaks, veal, pork, chicken and various cuts of meats. Every Sunday, my brother or I would have to climb inside that case and wash all the glass and climb back out.

With Bob and my father on the Oregon coast, 1927

Dad didn't fit of course, so he needed someone small to do the job, I guess. Maybe he figured we'd be able to get to spots that the adults couldn't get by just reaching inside.

Once cautions were taken for our safety, we were given the task to grind meat. We also took care of the chickens. We kept live chickens in the basement of the building in a coop, wired in from floor to ceiling. It was a big pen, probably fifty feet by twenty feet and fifteen feet tall, full of birds. Bobby and I had to feed the chickens and clean out their pen regularly, laying down fresh sawdust every Saturday.

When we were a bit older, Dad assigned us the job of slaughtering the chickens. He determined how many birds he thought we would need for the next day based on the day of the week, whether it was a holiday or there was a town event, the weather, and the time of year, and told us how many chickens to prepare. Dad might tell us to kill a half a dozen chickens or a dozen. One of the biggest days in Harry's Market was Saturday when the ladies would pick out meat for their Sunday supper. Bob and I would go into the basement and catch the chickens by the legs, hang them upside down, and cut their throats. Then we'd soak the carcasses in hot water and pick all the feathers off and dress them out. That's just the way life was.

My brother never did like to kill those chickens. He didn't think we should have to kill them. I defended my dad, I guess, or went along with the program. I cut most of the throats. Bob and I made the best of it, whistling, singing, and creating contests for speed-picking the feathers. We'd end up laughing in the hot, steaming basement with blood and feathers everywhere. Dad didn't pay us to do this or any of our jobs in the market. The understanding was, "Do it or else." After all, working in the butcher shop was a Mikkelson tradition, and our father was training us the way his father trained him.

Mikkelsons and the Butcher Tradition

My grandfather Mike Mikkelson with his bulldog

My grandfather, Michael Concord Mikkelson and his brother, my Uncle Roy, ran the first butcher shop in South St. Paul, Minnesota, called the Mikkelson Meat Company. (For a long time, Fern and I had the marble from their store in our kitchen, a beautiful piece still, since marble doesn't deteriorate.) They learned the trade in their home country of Denmark, where Grandpa Mike was born in 1863. He immigrated to the U.S. in 1882 and married my grandmother, Lena Roscoe Mikkelson (1867–1936) in the Evangelical Lutheran Church in Minnesota on October 20, 1888. My dad, Harry R. Mikkelson was born February 17, 1896, in St. Paul, Minnesota. Sometime in those years, Grandpa Mike became a chef on the Great Northern Railroad and then started the first meat market in South St. Paul, Minnesota in 1913, running it with his brother Roy. Thus the name: Mikkelson Brothers Meats. Later, it was renamed to Mikkelson and Son.

Dad started his responsibilities at the Mikkelson Brothers Meats shop about the same age that I started cleaning the showcase at our store, working with his dad and uncle after school and on Saturdays.

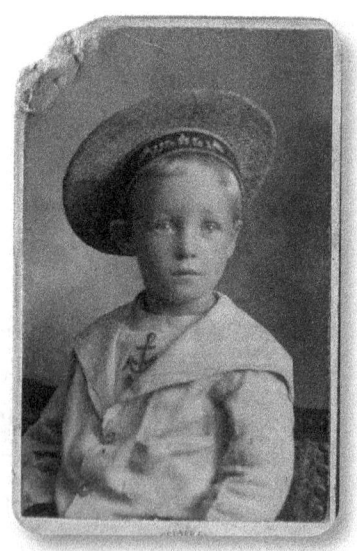

My father, Harry, circa 1900

Grandfataher and Great-Uncle Roy at the Mikkelson Brothers Meats shop, circa 1915
And below with my dad working there before WWI.

My father was the oldest of four with two sisters, Clara and Mabel and a brother named Roy, named after our uncle. Roy was the baby of the family. Along the way, while my father had many chores and responsibilities, Roy didn't have to do anything, but that didn't turn out well for him.

Along with the butcher shop, my grandfather had a side business renting out a carriage and four horses. Dad, as the oldest son, was assigned to help with that too. His job was to put the horses away, rub them down, care for them, and clean the stables, leaving the dung in perfect pyramid shapes, the way his father was taught in Denmark, and all that before my dad could go up to the house and eat.

My grandfather's carriage and two of the horses he rented out, circa 1906

He did as he was told, but what my father loved more than anything, starting as a child, was baseball. His dad would send him to Sunday school, but instead little Harry would go through the church and out the back door to where the baseball game was being played in South St. Paul, even though he knew if he got caught, he would get whipped.

My dad's brother, Roy with Grandpa Mike in St. Paul, late 1920s

Usually his sisters, Clara and Mabel, would tell on him, but he loved the game too much to stop. When he was old enough, he started playing in the semi pros, but this was interrupted by World War I.

My dad served in the Great War as an infantryman in the trenches in France, where it's clear he saw action and experienced the trauma of trench warfare, but he never talked about it. We knew about his service when we were kids only because our mother told us.

Three generations of Mikkelsons, Mike, Dad, me and Bob, circa 1926

I knew from school that the trenches were terrible, that if you stuck your head up, it'd get shot off. It wasn't much of a way to see France! According to Mom, Dad knew only three words in French. I think they were: Parlez-vous anglais?

From a book called *South St. Paul In the World War* (1919), we found out Dad was conscripted on May 22, 1918, and served as a private in Company D, 139th Infantry, 35th Division of the American Expeditionary Forces (A.E.F.) under the command of General John J. Pershing. The book says Dad was gassed in action.

My Dad's World War I Experience

From *The Story of the 139th Infantry* by Clair Kenamore, 1920, Guard Publishing Co., St. Louis, Missouri

Harry R. Mikkelson was among the infantrymen on Argonne Battlefield when they took Exermont. Here is an account of that day:

"A cold rain was falling steadily, and the hungry troops were soaked and chilled. The dreary untended field which lay between the northern edge of Montrebeau Wood and the town of Exermont was most desolate and repelling. The 35th Division was ordered to take Exermont and push as far beyond as it could…The division was a division in name only now. Brigade and Division Headquarters had almost ceased to function.

The effectives in charge of the direction of the troops were the regimental, battalion and company organizations. The 35th Division was, in effect, a number of small units, companies, battalions and regiments, waging little individual wars against a well-organized and well directed enemy. The higher command, which should have held together and directed the efforts of these smaller bodies as a unit, had lost its cohesion and had ceased to be a factor.

Exermont never was much of a town and the intense desire for it in the high command of the American Army was because of its position and the fact that it had been strongly fortified by the Germans. It blocked the way…

It was broad daylight when [Major Rieger] turned the last protecting corner of Montrebeau Wood and paced across the open ground. The field ahead of them was thick with machine gunners, placed there during the night, rifle fire from every protection was brought to bear on the attacking troops, artillery from three sides pounded them.

My father (left) and fellow soldier, 1918

> Rieger's men had been without warm food for four days. They were chilled with the rain and they were extremely tired because of the constant work of battle.
>
> So heavy was the fire from the front that men were seen to turn their faces from it while still advancing, as one will do in a gale of wind… Across the open field the worn infantry went, the losses growing heavier every minute. Across the little valley of Exermont and the creek. Fairly against the town they charged and they took it, grimly killing the enemy machine gunners at their guns and bombing the dug outs with awful thoroughness. Through the town they passed and to the heights beyond. There they dug a line and held it…and there the 2nd Battalion, the 139th Infantry and the 35th Division reached the height of their glory."

After his military service, Harry resumed work at the family's meat store but wanted to make a name for himself as a baseball player, touring with a team in Minnesota and North Dakota. No doubt he had his sights set on the St. Paul Saints, who represented his town in the American Association. (Roy Campanella, Leo Durocher, Lefty Gomez and Duke Snider were among some future major leaguers who played for the Saints.) I believe it was while he was touring to play baseball that he met my mom. She was in Minneapolis attending college at the time.

Even with his baseball, my father had to work a lot in the Mikkelson Meat store, his father being very strict. Michael Mikkelson was so strict, he wouldn't let his two girls get married. He thought nobody was good enough for them. Clara and Mabel ended up spinsters. It was horrible! They were both very nice-looking ladies and wonderful to be around. Every Christmas, Aunt Clara and Aunt Mabel would send Bob and me gifts from their home in St. Paul, a toy or something else fun. Grandpa left them some money and the house, which was worth something. Clara, the older of the two girls, also worked as a proofreader.

Without a work ethic, my dad's brother Roy never seemed to fully grow up. He had a little grocery store in St. Paul, but it failed. When my dad was managing Pfeiffer's Market, he said to Roy, "Well, you come out, and I'll find work for you." Roy and his wife Marge closed the grocery store and came out by train to live with us at our house in Albany, Oregon, and Roy started working at Harry's Meat Market. It became apparent even to us kids that he didn't know how to work. After a few months, my dad and mom had a "committee meeting" between the two of them, deciding Roy had to go. Dad put them on a train and sent them back to South St. Paul. I don't know what Roy did after that.

My father (top) and Uncle Roy when he was with us in Albany, 1932

Mother Alice at Harry's Market

While Roy was with us, he waited customers alongside my dad. A few years later, Bob was manning the counter while I fetched meat from the freezer and prepared and cut it in the back. A few other employees came and went. My mother worked at the shop regularly, manning the phone and keeping track of the accounts.

She was very capable and was essential to Harry's Market, keeping the accounts for the shop the entire time my father ran the place.

When customers came to the counter and ordered their hamburger or pork chops, whoever was waiting on them would write it down on a slip of paper in a sales book, weigh the meat and wrap it, or if it wasn't displayed or the proper weight, tell me or whoever else what was needed from the refrigerator or the back. When each order was complete, they would tear out the slip and put it on a spindle. If buying on credit, the customer simply left with their meat without paying for it. We kept charge accounts for our customers, a practice that no longer exists with today's credit cards and ATM machines.

My mother, on her stool by the phone, would collect all the orders from the spindle and register them into each customer's account. She kept all the accounts in a metal, fire-proof McCaskey, an old-time register. At the end of the week or month, the customers paid their bills. When they did—and it was usually the ladies—they'd pay their bill to my mother at the counter, chatting away with her if Mom had time. Mom was a great listener and very personable.

People could also phone in orders to Harry's Market to be picked up or delivered. My mom usually answered the calls. We were line 104. She'd write everything down and put the sales slip on the spindle for us to fulfill the order so it would be ready when the customer came in. Then, she'd put the sales slip into the McCaskey and post the sale. We made deliveries four times a day, at 8:00 a.m., 10:00 a.m., 2:00 p.m., and 4:00 p.m.

My dad had a poor memory for names, so when he was waiting on a return customer and couldn't remember her name and knew he should, he would ask, "Now how do you spell that name?" One time he did this and the customer's answer was, "J-O-N-E-S." Bob and I had a good laugh.

My mother always said, "Now remember, treat your daddy nice." We did. He loved us, but sometimes he treated us badly.

With my father, mother and Bob, 1928

"You damn little farts, get out!" he'd say. That's the way his dad treated him. He didn't know anything else. Sometimes if my brother and I stopped for a moment in the shop to talk about something, my dad would take ten steps back towards us, beside the walk-in cooler and cuss at us, "You little bastards, get working!" My mother, sitting by the phone, heard him of course and said to him many times, "I wish you wouldn't do that." He was a veteran of World War I, and as such, she sometimes made excuses for him, but not always, not when he cussed a lot.

Otherwise, my father was a man who didn't have time for small talk, and we didn't have much communication with him, but he worked very hard. I didn't have a very good relationship with Dad, because I was pretty much afraid of him, but the same time, I'm glad I had a good tough dad. I learned to work hard and take on obligations.

Dad loved to drink, and we knew he wouldn't change. He never went down to the liquor store on his own to buy a bottle and bring it home. He wouldn't dare do that, but he'd drink around the market, hiding a bottle here or there.

We furnished meat for the Greyhound Bus Depot restaurant, where all the buses came and went. Jim Christie, who ran the Depot restaurant drank too. He'd bring a bottle down and meet my dad in the alley across from the meat market next to the post office or my dad would have him into the back room of the shop. My mom figured out something was wrong. One time she walked into the backroom, and there they were, my dad and Jim Christie, drinking right out of the bottle. My mom was a little gal, not more than 100 pounds, but that didn't stop her. She grabbed that bottle and poured it out. My dad was really upset, but he didn't say anything. He knew he couldn't. He respected ladies, and he loved her a lot.

Harry Mikkelson in Albany

My dad was involved in the community. He was a member of the Masons, Elks, Rotary and American Legion organizations for many years. He helped found the American Legion Junior Baseball program in Albany in 1940.

My dad and mom were members of the Presbyterian Church of Albany for more than 50 years. They were well known throughout the community for their leadership and involvement in a variety of worthwhile ventures.

Play Hard

Even though we worked at an early age, our childhood wasn't all work. We played hard too. Albany, Oregon, was a wonderful place to grow up, so much so, I raised my own children there.

For our first three years in Albany, we settled into a rental home on Fourth Avenue. The main form of transportation for the Mikkelson boys in the early years were our tricycles.

Me, 1928

Bob and me in Oregon, circa 1929

At first, Bob and I were limited to the sidewalks on half a block where Fourth Street met Ferry Street. Pastor Daniel Poling and his family kept track of our antics on the Ferry Street side while Pastor Rex Dallas kept watch on Fourth Street. We had a lot of fun riding into our church across the way at 330 5th Avenue. In those days, it was kept unlocked, as most community buildings and houses were. Built in 1913, First Presbyterian (now called United Presbyterian Church) was a big, castle-like stone building with stained-glass windows. We called it the Stone Pile. Inside the congregation gathered in a wide circular nave in pews separated by two parallel aisles that sloped down toward the altar. Bobby and I and our friend Paul Stocker would gleefully ride down the aisles, walk the trikes back up, and do it again, over and over.

For the most part, Bob and I were considered "cute, clean and well dressed." However, the former society editor of the *Democrat-Herald*, Ianthe Smith, loved to tell us how she observed Bob and me one day following our mother down the street, pushing and shoving each other until our mother turned around. Under her gaze, we became immediate angels. When she turned away again, we resumed our rough play.

Because we were close in age and Mom dressed us alike, we were often mistaken for twins. I especially remember our matching raincoats. We usually corrected people, but the misconception was to our advantage when the Twin Roundup took place in Bryant Park and awarded us with free ice cream cones and other goodies.

The county courthouse was located across the street from us on SW 4th Avenue. They didn't lock the door to that building either. A three-story building featuring a tall clock tower, probably seven-stories high (It has since been torn down and rebuilt), we rode our tricycles inside it too. By ages five and six, we started climbing the stairs to the top of the tower where I'd throw unripe walnuts, still with their green covers, at people passing by.

With our mother in the matching raincoats she made us, circa 1928

Linn County Courthouse, 1920s

When my mom found out I was doing that, she made me promise that I'd only throw dried walnuts without the shell. She didn't want me to hurt anybody. I don't think I could have; I didn't throw very well at that age. I did what she instructed though. We were pretty well-behaved boys.

Inside another part of the county courthouse was the town jail. Our friend, Sheriff Shelton lived with his wife in an upstairs apartment above the jail. That was interesting to us, because we saw policeman and the various characters that went in and out of there. One night, there was a jail break. We awoke to gunfire, thrilled at the excitement of it all. Our mother wouldn't let us go outside, of course.

Fun Around the Corner on 10th Avenue

About the time Bob was entering grade school, we moved to 637 West 10th Avenue. Albany's population was still not much more than 5,000 throughout most of my childhood and young adulthood. The town grew, but not fast (the current population is about 52,000). Despite being the county seat, only the downtown streets were paved in the late 1920s and early 1930s as I recall (with bitulithic pavement), along with only one street in our residential area, 9th Avenue. The other streets were mostly gravel at that time. I don't know why 9th was paved and not the rest. Perhaps because of the influence of my friend's daddy who was a chiropractor and had money and lived on 9th Street and owned one of the only private automobiles in town during the Great Depression years. At least I remember it being the only one at the time. Having the train station and with money tight and gasoline rationed, I suppose most people in Albany felt they didn't need or couldn't afford a car or the gas, which was fifteen cents a gallon or so.

The doctor's car was a Chrysler Airflow, one of the first streamlined vehicles in the U.S. (manufactured from 1934 to 1937). Everybody in town loved looking at that car, but the doctor didn't allow us kids to hang around it much.

He had two sons close to our age. With 9th Avenue being paved and close to where we lived at 637 West Tenth, that was where we all met to play almost every evening in summer and after school until the parents told us to go home. We roller-skated there, boys and girls together, wearing the old metal skates that you would buckle on to the bottom of your shoes. And we'd play roller hockey. We made our own hockey sticks from branches of the willow trees that grew a short way up along the mill stream. They had natural hooks on them, making them perfect for the purpose.

With my father, his mother-in-law, Sarah, and cousins in North Dakota

We'd cut them and let them age for quite a while until the green wood dried and turned gray-brown. For a puck, we used a Carnation can that we'd jump on to stamp it down flat. We also played hide and seek, which was called Olly, Olly, Oxen Free back then. We played in that manner almost every day, and it was a lot of fun.

School Days

Our elementary school, Maple School, was only three blocks away from home in an old two-story building with an irresistible fire escape slide running down one side. The slide—designed for emergency escapes and not for little boys' fun—was long, spanning all the way from the top floor down to the ground past an above-ground basement. Bob and I would climb out the window at the top of the slide and come streaking down sitting on old waxed bread wrappers to add speed and danger.

During after school hours, we also liked climbing all over these giant wood piles in the yard (This was not allowed during school!). The wood was used to heat the building by burning it in a large furnace, with a tower chimney releasing the smoke. The wood, sold to the school very cheaply by the local logging companies, consisted of slabs seven and eight feet long, all the bark removed. They were stacked out in front of the school in a pile eight to ten feet high and about fifty or seventy-five yards long. We especially enjoyed playing pretend games on those.

To get to Maple School and back home each day, we usually walked beside the Big Ditch. Our yard on 10th Avenue butted up against a wire fence, on the other side of which was a thirty-foot wide canal, perfectly straight, dug by hand in the 1870s and dammed to support the mills and provide Albany with its water supply. It runs 18 miles, branching out from the South Santiam River flowing down the mountains through Lebanon and across farmland to the treatment plant at Third and Vine, built in 1912.

Bob and I could almost spit in the canal from our bedroom. We were never supposed to go over the fence into that water, but we wouldn't dare anyway. The current was strong and when we were little, we didn't know how to swim.

In my first years at Maple School, Bob and I went home for lunch each day since we lived close by, but it was a real treat if we could carry a lunch and have longer play time at break with our friends.

With our teachers and Bob beside Maple School, 1930

I vaguely remember when we were in fifth or sixth grade the school adding a cafeteria that offered cold sandwiches and the like. That was in the new building. Maple School was razed (January 1936) and a new, more modern building opened in its place the following September.

Twice a day every day, in the morning and after lunch, rain or shine, all the students assembled outside and strutted into the building to a march by Johann Strauss or John Philip Sousa played on an old phonograph record. If it was necessary to discipline a student—and of course that never happened to the Mikkelson boys!—that student sat on the bench in the hall while all the rest of the students marched past, a rather humiliating experience.

We didn't have very many kids in the school, three or four hundred in the whole school, kindergarten through sixth grade. Back then, students started school in either September or January. I started in January and continued on with the same mid-year class, which tended to be smaller than the fall group, until I was skipped a grade.

Little Billy Jumps Down and Moves Up

My second-grade teacher, Mrs. Frazier, kept "little Billy" in after school once in a while because of a little misbehaving. One time it was because I chased a mouse around the room in the middle of class.

One afternoon, I decided I didn't want to be in detention anymore. While I sat dejected in the classroom, which was on the second floor, Mrs. Frazier stepped out of the room for a moment. We had a big window in each classroom that we would open and close depending on the temperature. I raised the window, lifted myself onto the ledge, and jumped out, about twelve feet down to the ground below, and off I ran. She came back in the room just in time to see me jump.

"Billy, Billy, get back here!" she yelled from the window, but I kept going, running along the Big Ditch all the way home. The teacher wisely didn't exacerbate the penalty. She just shook her head and talked to my mother. She loved my mother and was sympathetic with her.

Just a few weeks later come January, when I was supposed to start third grade, the school skipped me to the fourth grade. I guess Mrs. Frazier had enough of me! Actually, she seemed to like me and perhaps thought I was bored and not challenged enough. Being a happy-go-lucky child, I suppose she thought I was cute, or she saw something in me. When I walked by, she liked to shake my hand. It felt so tiny in hers. She would put her face down next to mine and say, "Billy, don't you ever lose that smile." But the decision to move me up definitely had an effect.

My fourth grade class after being skipped a grade. I'm third from right, third row. Bob is second row, 5th from left, 1931.

The Youngest, But Not the Last

I grew up pretty rapidly after I skipped a grade. In a way, I lost a year of my life. In another way, I was lucky. It was easy for me to catch up with the fourth graders academically, including my brother, with whom I went through all the grades after that including high school. Academics for me were just mechanical. You just do it.

The social situation, however, was more of a challenge. Being younger than all the rest, I felt the need to prove myself. It helped that Bob and I were among the larger boys in the class at that age and that we got along fine. We had our lunch at the same time, generally went home at the same time, and didn't squabble a lot. But being younger, I felt I had to work a lot harder than others for the respect of my peers.

Mikkelson Self-Defense

Periodically, we found ourselves in disagreements with our classmates, which sometimes resulted in a fight. Dad thought we should learn to defend ourselves and bought us boxing gloves. A couple times, he lectured to us and demonstrated the art of self-defense. Then Bob and I were expected to box each other. Inevitably, one of us would give the other a good blow that would bring on tears. Our mother was not keen on this activity. However, if one Mikkelson brother was in trouble, the other would be there to assist, and we were not subjected to many fights after that.

Dad also thought we should be able to wrestle. With a mattress placed in the middle of the living room floor, we took lessons from a friend of Dad's. It didn't last long but perhaps it gave us a little more physical confidence. Again, our mother wasn't thrilled about it.

Mikkelson Sunday Morning Baseball Workouts

My brother Bob, remembering the details in a speech he wrote for me in 1998, said:

"The Sunday morning workouts on the diamond were seldom fun. Dad would hit ground balls to us with verbal instructions and criticisms, and we knew what he expected, but somehow the ball always hit a pebble and bounced into us or over our heads. It was not fun—rather like the boxing lessons. Dad really thought that baseball was great, and he was a very good player. I'm not sure that either Bill or I measured up to his standards. However, we always tried to be athletes with greater and lesser degrees of success. Bill became a respectable first baseman, and I chose third base."

The Baseball Workout

Baseball was a big part of growing up a Mikkelson. Dad continued to play semi-pro ball throughout my childhood, on Albany's top team, Albany Linn County, Oregon, ALCO (American Legion Club of Oregon), playing second base. He was pretty good. He played in games every Sunday afternoon that he could, mostly in town but sometimes traveling to a neighboring town for a game, never that far away though. Nobody traveled much in those days.

Those semi-pro baseball games were a form of popular entertainment for the townsfolk and well-attended. The baseball field was really just a dirt lot that the men cleaned up and raked, using white powder to mark the baselines. But it did have a homerun fence beyond the outfield, and the stands held around 150 people. Each weekend that he played, my father earned twenty-five or fifty cents. We usually sat in the stands watching him play.

With my dad's love of the

game, he wanted us to be good baseball players too. Bats, balls and gloves were early gifts. Since Sundays were the only day of the week that the butcher shop was closed, every Sunday morning, Dad would take Bob and me out to the diamond to practice. We had to throw, catch grounders, field fly balls, and take some swings—whether we wanted to or not! These mandatory practices weren't much fun. Luckily, we enjoyed playing in games, and both of us got to be pretty good as a result of the regular practice.

The End of Boxing for Bob

After school and in evenings, we'd also play baseball with our friends on the diamond. When it was just us kids, we'd play with the same ball forever and usually had only one or two bats at our disposal. It was there that Bob's boxing "career" came to an end.

One day, we had a game going with about a dozen boys and a couple girls, including Catherine Arthur and Beulah Kenagy—Beulah, that's a name you don't hear anymore! Catherine was getting ready for her turn at bat, taking practice swings, and my brother walked right in the path of the bat. It hit him squarely in the face and broke his nose. It was quite a scene. As a result, he wasn't permitted to do any more boxing.

Boxing in the Community Ring

Without Bob to box with, I moved to the community ring when I was six years old. I think part of my motivation was to please my dad. The men there would pull a rope taut between us two boys in the ring. It was tied to the backs of chairs on either end to keep us from full body contact. We'd just tap each other under the rope at first. As we got older, the rope between us was removed. We'd pound each other with little, teeny gloves. I don't remember receiving any more coaching after that. Mostly we watched the adults fight in the community ring and modeled ourselves after them.

Bob and I (left) posing in our boxing helmets, circa 1931

At home, a boxing glove hung on a hook on the living room wall. My father told my mother, and then she told us, that the glove was used by the boxer who knocked out the champion of Canada. I thought that was pretty impressive.

Treehouse Adventures

Our backdoor neighbors, the Bates family, had five boys and three girls. One boy, Clarence Bates, was close to our age, a tall kid and a good athlete. The entire family was athletic. We played a lot of pretend games together with Clarence. We'd be Tarzan of the Apes, underground adventurers, African explorers, and cowboys like Hoot Gibson, a rodeo star and popular actor in Westerns of the day. We rode home-made broomstick horses, made spears out of willow branches, and dug an underground tunnel, covering it with boards and dirt—a scare for Mom when she noticed the smoke coming out of the underground fireplace we had concocted.

Clarence's two eldest brothers were in college at Washington State where they both played football. One summer when they were home from college, they decided to build a tree house for all of us in our big maple tree. The tree was perfect for a treehouse with thick, spread-out limbs. The Bates brothers' construction featured three separate "bedrooms," one for each of us, with ropes for ladders. They used big timbers, 6 x12 and 20 feet long, sturdy enough that nobody worried about the floors caving in. We built sides and a roof, but they refused to keep the rooms dry on rainy days.

The tree house became our fort, from which we would defend ourselves from other kids in the neighborhood. We had great battles. For bombs, we collected fireplace ashes and orange wrappers. Everyone had wood-burning fireplaces in their homes in those days, so ashes were plentiful. Oranges in those days came wrapped in tissue paper. We'd pour ashes into a tissue until it was full, tie up the edges with a string, and throw them from our tree house at invaders that got too close. If you got hit by an ash bomb, Boosh! It was a mess.

When the big maple leaves came down in the fall, we burned them in a pile and cooked potatoes over the fire, usually burning the tubers, but they still tasted good.

There was a big fir tree between our house and the Bates' as well, at least 100 feet tall, and the college guys would climb way up the tree, holding on to the trunk with their knees, and wave at us. This was a skill that many young men in Albany learned so they could compete in the annual Timber Festival. It took place every Fourth of July from 1941 to 2000 to celebrate Independence Day and to focus on the region's timber industry with competitive logrolling, wood chopping, and cross-cut sawing. There was also a royal court—consisting of princesses from Albany—a parade, and a fireworks display. It was a fun tradition.

No More Piano Lessons

Because she loved playing the piano, Mother wanted Bobby and I to take piano lessons. When I was about seven years old and Bob was eight, we started taking lessons from a neighbor, Justin Miller. The lessons were twenty-five cents apiece, as I recall. Another boy, Don Beight also took lessons from Justin Miller and since each lesson was a half hour, the two that were waiting would spend it in his front yard wrestling. Our mother could never understand how we could get so dirty taking a music lesson!

But we soon discovered that learning piano was more about practicing daily than going to the lessons. It wasn't long, probably less than a year, before Bob put his foot down and said, "I'm not going to practice anymore." I stuck with it a little longer than Bob did. Mom finally tired of our complaining when I was in the third grade, saying something like, "Well, if you don't want to practice, I'm through with you." We never came close to achieving our mother's skill level, but we did learn a great appreciation for music.

My mom continued to play though, so we had live music in the house which was marvelous to me. She taught Sunday school and directed the church choir. Occasionally, before Harry's Market, she gave a lesson to someone now and then in our home, she never charged for it. Or if she did, it was for twenty-five cents a lesson or something like that.

Later, when I had kids of my own, Mom oversaw their piano practices every Saturday so they were prepared for their lessons with Sara Ella Worley.

My Mother, Alice

My mother was a special lady. Alice Pansy Greiner Mikkelson was born on May 19, 1897, the ninth of eleven children, and grew up in Bottineau, North Dakota. She never liked her middle name and didn't use it much. She was a pretty lady, just five-foot-two, whose hair turned gray when she was still rather young. Everybody just thought she was marvelous. She was just so sweet to everybody. If you had trouble at home, you could tell her anything, and she'd listen, just like she did with the ladies that came into Harry's Market.

She never talked to us about her upbringing really, but you find out things now and then by listening, especially going into your teenage years. And other members of our family took on the research and writing of the Greiner family history, which helped Bob and me to understand her past.

Her father, my grandfather James Greiner (1853-1925), was the third child of four to William and Mary Ann Greiner who settled in Minneapolis, Minnesota, in 1857, a year before it became a state.

James' father made a good living in the new territory running grist and lumber mills and farming. At an early age, James worked in the mill with his father and uncle learning the trade before branching off on his own, along with brother Morris. In 1878, James and Morris rented a mill on Bear Creek called the Tunnel Mill, in which they milled mostly wheat and corn. Minneapolis was known then as Mill City, St. Anthony Falls and its surrounding rivers providing the power for multiple mills (Today, Tunnel Mill has been restored into a blacksmith and traditional iron work mill).

In 1882, Grandpa James fell in love with a lovely young woman named Sarah Orilla Turner, whose father was a farmer and Union veteran of the Civil War. They married in 1882 in Summer, Minnesota. That same year, their first child was born and James and Sarah moved into North Dakota Territory where they obtained a homestead and built a little shack about four miles south of the old town of Bottineau. The territory had just opened up for settlement the year before, and James swiftly became a leader in

James Newton Greiner, my grandfather, 1882

Sarah Orilla Turner Greiner, my grandmother, 1882

the burgeoning community, appointed as county treasurer in 1885-86 (while North Dakota was still a territory) and serving as County Commissioner. The family, practicing Presbyterians, supported the building of the first church in the area. (Their efforts and success were helped by the Homestead Act passed in 1862. Farmers were given a piece of land in return for utilizing and settling on that land. A section of land, as defined by the Northwest Ordinance of 1787, was 640 acres and cost $200.)

Bottineau, North Dakota, 1890s

In 1883, James was able to get a new house built for his family at 323 5th Street in Bottineau, which was good since he and Sarah proceeded to have eleven children in all. Shortly after moving into the new house, he opened a feed store with an undertaking business and funeral parlor at the rear of the store, and interesting combination. James had a real entrepreneurial spirit, venturing into multiple business enterprises, many a great success.

In 1890, James took over as the grain buyer and agent for the Minneapolis and Northern Elevator Company. His grain elevator, located a few short blocks from their home, had a capacity of 35,000 bushels. He owned a livery stable in Bottineau, a busy place until 1906 when the automobile took over. Above the Greiner Feed Store, the family ran a combination roller skating rink and dance hall, a popular gathering spot in town. He owned and operated the Bottineau Opera House, which held close to 600 people. It was lighted with lanterns, had three dressing rooms backstage, a large stage, and a pit for the orchestra. Drinking was not allowed during performances.

My mother's childhood home in Bottineau

My mom spent much of her childhood helping at the family businesses. Along with her sisters, she would usher and sell tickets for the Opera House while her little brothers Earl (Uncle Jack) and Dewey (sometimes known as Dukes) sold the popcorn their mother made for the shows. Sometimes after school, Jack and Dewey would sneak into the empty opera house and reenact their favorite characters on the stage for a make-believe audience. However, their older brother Noble actually played an extra with some of the various summer stock companies that came through from California. He loved the stage. In *The Greiners of Amityville, Pennsylvania, 1700-1900*, Alice recalls seeing Shakespeare's Taming of the Shrew and Stevenson's *Dr. Jekyll and Mr. Hyde*, among other productions. Minstrel and Vaudeville shows would also pass through as they became popular in the first two decades of the 20th Century. When they became available (1891 through 1927), silent movies were also shown at the Opera House, and Alice played the piano for the movies. She would sometimes get so interested in the picture that she hardly paid any attention to what she was playing.

The Greiner girls all took music lessons and played the piano. Nellie also played the violin and piccolo. William played a horn in the Bottineau Town Band.

The Greiner family continued to be active in the Presbyterian Church, attending four times on Sundays, starting with Sunday school and the morning church service, then the evening short service followed by a meeting of the Young Peoples Christian Endeavor. Afterwards, the Greiner youngsters would often bring friends home and they would gather around the piano and sing. James always requested his favorite song, the "Battle Hymn of the Republic." While the music was going on, some of the other kids would listen while playing games at the dining room table, and all would eat Sarah's freshly made popcorn and fudge and sometimes pull taffy.

My mother, Alice Greiner, circa 1911

Alice and her sister Ada took turns playing the organ in the church, which had to be pumped backstage by hand. When Alice practiced, Dewey and Earl were supposed to be doing the pumping, but sometimes they'd forget, and the organ would run out of air. Alice also harmonized with her sisters in the occasional special vocal number during services.

In between services on Sunday afternoons, a favorite activity for the Greiner family in summer was to hitch up their horse to the buggy and go for a ride up into the Turtle Mountains just north of town where they would pick berries when in season, and nearly always James would pick a bouquet of fresh flowers for Sarah.

Sarah was always at home when the children arrived from school often having surprises for them like a big panful of doughnuts or freshly baked rolls. They had their household routines too. Monday was washday, Tuesday ironing. No one had whiter, cleaner clothes than Sarah Greiner, according to her children.

Christmas was always a memorable event with the singing of Christmas carols and a crackling fire using wood collected from the huge piles of firewood stored behind the house that the boys cut, split and piled during the summer months. They would also cut and cart home a Christmas tree from the mountains that the family would cover with ornaments, tinsel and real candles. Christmas dinner included roast turkey, mashed potatoes, gravy, turnips, puddings and pies.

Alice continued this tradition in the Mikkelson household where Christmases were always special and memorable.

Sports were important in the lives of the Greiner family. Alice, along with sisters Nellie, Ada, and Thirza played tennis and basketball. A challenge in those days for girls was the requirement to play the sport in mid-length skirts. Ada and Nellie played on Bottineau High's champion basketball team of 1910-11. Alice, an outstanding player, was the center for her team. All the boys played basketball, baseball and football. Jack and Dewey played on the same high school team for a couple years, Dewey as forward and both lettered in all three sports. Dewey's first love, however, was tennis, and he often teamed up in matches with Alice or with Ada and Nellie. Luther was skilled in bowling and roller skating. In 1907, Alice's brother Noble played baseball for the North Dakota School of Forestry. The team was referred to by sports writers as the "nine iron men," because with only nine players, they all played every game. Jack went on to become captain of Moorhead State Teacher's College baseball team while attending classes there (specializing in Industrial Arts, primarily Woodwork) and went on to play semi-pro ball in various parts of North Dakota and the West Coast, as well as in the old Dunning League in Southern Saskatchewan. He played shortstop and second base and was a solid hitter. All during that time, he taught woodshop and coached football, basketball and baseball.

Bottineau High basketball team, 1915
Alice Greiner (front center)

Noble Greiner in front of tent on homestead, Alberta, Canada, 1908

Noble was the first to move to Canada in 1907, lured by the opening of new frontier. At only 18 years old, he found himself on a homestead in Enchant, Alberta, where he faced the challenges of pioneer farming and endured the extreme cold and loneliness of the long winters and the heat of the summer in nothing but a tent at first, then eventually in the luxury of a wood shack.

William was the next to go north in 1908. He acquired a homestead six miles east of Vantage and 65 miles south of Moose Jaw where he built himself a sod shack as he started farming. Luther joined him and two years later, they had earned enough money for lumber to build a barn and wooden house. Thirza, the eldest sibling in the Greiner family, also ended up in Saskatchewan where she worked as a nurse and met her husband Tom.

In 1915, their father James decided to join the boys up north. He traded his feed store and elevator in Bottineau for land at Wauchope, Saskatchewan, then the following year took on a homestead near his son's.

But within a short time, they all ended up in the Vantage district a very small, rural hamlet in Sutton Rural Municipality No. 103, Saskatchewan, Canada, where William and Luther had settled. My mother was seventeen. With Jack and Dewey still in secondary school, however, Sarah stayed behind in North Dakota. I wonder what my mother thought when she visited the family in Vantage that first time. There were only a few houses in town. There's no one living in Vantage today. It's just fields and granaries. Shortly after World War I, the boys helped move their mother Sarah from North Dakota to Saskatchewan to be with the rest of the family while my mom, Jack and Dewey sought higher education and careers in the states.

My mother's ambition was to teach school so she went to Minneapolis to attend the same private teachers' college that her sister Ada had attended just a few years earlier. Her brothers William and Luther paid for her education in exchange for a summer of work on their farm. She stayed at her Aunt Kate Keatley's place first then moved into an apartment with Ada. Nellie also lived with them for a time while she started her nursing career.

After graduation, Mom taught kindergarten in Aikley, Minnesota, then later at a school in St. Paul. She also spent a year in Saskatchewan, Canada, on the homestead with the family. During that year she taught school at Hilton, a few miles east of the town of Vantage, Saskatchewan.

Nellie had known my dad and his sisters for some time and suggested to Alice one evening that they go over to the Mikkelsons' and play the piano. Harry's father, Michael, had a bulldog.

Nellie taking her three sisters for a ride. (left to right)
Nellie, Thirza, Alice and Ada, 1908

During my mother's first visit, whenever the young folks began to play and sing around the piano, the dog would start to howl.

My mother was terribly grieved when Nellie died in December 1919. After getting her nursing degree in Chicago, she practiced in Minnesota, helping people suffering from the Spanish influenza and contracted the flu from one of her patients.

Eventually my grandparents moved back to Minneapolis and were living there when my grandfather James died on June 11, 1925. My mother, with us two little babies in tow, stayed with her mother

My mother, circa 1920

to support her. That's why we were living there before we moved out west. Grandma Sarah moved back to Vantage after we left for Oregon.

Alice Pansy Greiner Mikkelson was probably the ideal mom. She dressed well. She had good manners. She was very kind to people. She always tried to serve, to do something for somebody. And she loved us very much. We had to eat our spinach. She didn't cuddle and kiss a lot, but that was often the way back then. Affection was never apparent with Daddy. I never saw her kiss him. She did hug me around the neck now and then though, and she was there for all of us and worked really hard.

The Greiner Family

From: *The Greiners of Amityville, Pennsylvania, 1700-1900* by M.L. Greiner (1981)

My mother, Alice's family, the Greiners were of "Pennsylvania Dutch" heritage, which is the term used to describe early German settlers to the colony of Pennsylvania.

The first Greiners to arrive in America were Johann Dietrich Griner (becoming John Theodore Greiner in the new country) and his wife Dorothy. Both grew up in the Old German Empire State of Lower Palatinate. Along with thousands of Palatines, they migrated to the American colonies in search of peace and freedom from war. The Nine Year's War (1689–97) is often considered to be the first global war in history. Also known as the War of the Grand Alliance and the War of the League of Augsburg, it had ravaged their homeland and unrest continued into the 1700s.

The Greiners arrived on September 30, 1732 in the Philadelphia harbor aboard the ship Dragon under the command of Captain Charles Hargrave. They were among 185 Palatines to make the voyage.

In the year prior to his arrival, John had secured two hundred acres of land for 32 pounds, thirteen shillings, and four pence in what would become Berks County, Pennsylvania. The Greiners struggled at first as they worked the land and built a modest shack-like home. Like most German immigrants in the area, their house included an outdoor oven to bake bread and an outdoor furnace with an iron kettle to make soap, lard and apple butter and to boil clothes on washday. Overtime, they built themselves a bigger house as well as a barn made of logs, modeled after those built by the Swedes who had settled there some years before.

Being Lutheran, they helped support the building of the first Lutheran church in the area, a log church in New Storeville in 1753. It would eventually be known as St. Paul's Church of Amityville and is still in operation today. John Theodoric Greiner passed away in 1765.

Like his father, John Jr. was a farmer (born 17?, died 1788). John Jr.'s eldest son Philip (my great-great-great grandfather, 1754-1823) served as a private in the American Revolution in 1781 and 1782, stationed with the Berks County Militia. Like his father and grandfather, he was a farmer.

Philip's son Samuel Newton Greiner (my great-great grandfather, 1789-1874) started off as a farmer as well, but found his calling as a carpenter in Pottstown, Pennsylvania.

Samuel Greiner, circa 1960

His son, my great grandfather, William James Greiner (1825 to 1910), began learning his father's craft of carpentry when he was 16 years old. Westward expansion was sweeping the nation, and in 1849, the territory of Minnesota was created with land and opportunities opening up there. In 1857, William, his wife Mary Ann Garber Greiner (married in 1950), and their four surviving young children (their first died at the age of four) made the long and tedious journey by rail, horse and riverboat up the Mississippi along with thousands of settlers from the east. They found a new home in Minneapolis, Minnesota, where William's brother David had built a saw and grist mill the year before.

William Greiner, circa 1875

William bought a half interest in the mill on Bear Creek in Jordan Township. The mill, powered by an eleven-foot fall of water, was said to turn out feed and high-quality flour. During the winter of 1857, it had to be run day and night so it wouldn't freeze.

They sawed over 90,000 feet of lumber during that period. After 1878 when the dam washed out (also the year of the great Washburn A. Mill explosion in Menneapolis that destroyed most of the mill district), William turned his enterprise to farming and stock raising, using oxen to plow the land and sowing the grain and corn by hand and in this way made a good life for himself and his family in the sparsely populated village of Washington.

William and Mary Ann's third child, James Newton Greiner (1853-1925) was my grandfather who settled in Minneapolis, Minnesota.

Grandmother

We paid extended visits to our grandmother and cousins in Vantage a few times, mostly so my mother could spend time with her mother, Sarah. Mother was concerned about her with my grandfather gone and all of my mom's brothers and sisters living elsewhere except for Uncle William and Uncle Luther and their families.

Talk about western and rural! Vantage had wooden-slat sidewalks that Bob and I would run up and jump off into the dirt street. There wasn't any gravel, let alone paving. When it rained, we'd go barefoot and play in the mud in the street. There was no indoor plumbing either. The town had one city well for drinking water. Bobby and I were too young to haul water, but other members of the family did. And they collected rain water at the house as well. At the end of the main street, which was only about a hundred yards long to begin with, was the community toilet.

Nobody had a toilet at their house. The outhouse was pretty private though, a three-holer with seats carved out of 2 x 6s mounted on 4 x 4s. Probably about 30 households shared the community toilet. You didn't dare lock yourself in! For nighttime, in my grandmother's house, we just had chamber pots.

My uncle had a grain farm there, and the granary was all that supported the small town. That was the industry. When we visited there, we learned that muskrats were digging holes in his grain field, much to his chagrin. He told my cousin and Bob and me that if we caught and killed them, he'd give us a penny a tail. Sometimes we'd make five or six cents. I must've been around five years old the first time we did this. In the store, candy bars cost a penny a piece. So, five or six muskrats meant five or six candy bars. Not bad! The Stock Market had crashed, starting the Great Depression, and it was nearing its worst at that time, but being a child, I wasn't fully aware of its effects. I do remember my family really counting pennies, and a penny was worth quite a bit of money. To me, though, it meant a candy bar.

My grandmother Sarah in Vantage

For a short time in 1930, Grandma came out to Oregon to live with us. It was uncomfortable, I suppose, living alone, and my mother felt sorry for her. But either Albany or living with her daughter and son-in-law or being away from Vantage didn't suit her. I don't know what it was, but she got god-awful grumpy, complaining and moaning constantly. It wasn't long before my father declared, "We've got to get her out of here," and she returned to Canada, and we made our way to Vantage for several more extended stays. Grandma died in Moose Jaw, Saskatchewan on September 26, 1948.

Uncle Jack and Uncle Dewey

Because our family worked six days a week, we didn't see my uncles and aunts and cousins in Oregon much. We visited Uncle Jack and his family in McMinnville on some holidays and vacations, and Uncle Dewey and his family about once a month. My mother always tried to get us together.

Another factor making it difficult was that we didn't have a car. Mr. Pfeiffer, the owner of the meat market, would loan my daddy the company pick-up truck. Bobby and I would ride in the back of the pickup the entire twenty miles on curvy and narrow roads to Salem to see Uncle Dewey and his family on our monthly visit. One time, we were on our way and driving through a town when my dad took a sharp turn, and Bob was thrown out of the back of the pickup onto the pavement. I looked back, and there he was, lying in the gutter. My dad quickly put on the brakes, and we ran to check him out. Luckily, he didn't get hurt, and we got him back in the pickup and went on to Salem.

My parents knew a couple who had a granary mill, and they owned an Oldsmobile that they shared with others in the community. That was really something. They kept it in the mill covered up so it remained clean and shiny, and my parents rode with them in that sometimes.

Uncle Jack

Uncle Dewey, when I knew him, was a manager of the Salem Navigation Company, the admiral of a small Navy, as it were, a bunch of boats and their operations. They had a paper mill in Salem, and the paper had to go to Portland to be shipped to Japan or elsewhere down the river. We'd watch it being loaded onto the ferries with Uncle Dewey, handsome in his vest and suit.

Interestingly enough, at Oregon City there was a forty-foot waterfall. These boats had to be transported past the falls. They used locks. The boat would enter the calm water of a lock, the operator would shut the gate and flood it and float the ferry out the other side.

Uncle Jack was supremely good looking. Otherwise, he was just an ordinary guy. He was highly respected, however, and always liked to tell jokes. I saw him quite regularly when I was a young adult. With McMinnville being sixty miles away, we didn't get to see Uncle Jack as often as Dewey.

The rest of my mom's siblings were all in Saskatchewan.

Acquiring Tim

Earning spending money became important to me when I was seven years old. Luckily, friends of my parents came to depend on me to mow their lawn every other Saturday or some exact repeating time, and I'd mow it beautifully with their hand-pushed mower and then edge it. They had to provide the mower; I didn't own one. It would take me at least an hour or two, and they paid me twenty-five cents and a bottle of homemade root beer. I had a great use for that twenty-five cents!

One of the things I wanted money for was to buy a dog. I really wanted a dog, and our family had never owned one. I started going to the Saturday auction looking for one. Every Saturday, the town auction was held under the bridge that goes over the Calapooia River in downtown. Merchants would auction off cattle, pigs, bicycles, dogs, tools, all kinds of stuff.

One day after mowing, I went to the auction with coins jingling in my pocket and, standing on the lowest rung of the fence that separated the animals from the crowd, watched the undertakings carefully through the wooden rail bars. That's when I saw this little dog, and I knew he was the one. The auctioneer was a friend of our family, and his son was a friend of mine too, and I told him that was the puppy for me. When it came time to auction off the little mutt, I bid twenty-five cents, and he wouldn't let anybody else bid on it. I went home with the dog. This was a surprise to my parents, but it was fine with them, as long as I took care of him. I named him Tim, and he lived seventeen years. It was fun to run around with Tim. Of course, later on when we were busy in high school and then college and I was away in-flight training, we had to connect his collar to a long leash on the clothesline so he could run back and forth during the daytime and get enough exercise, but Tim was a great dog.

Bicycles and Paper Routes

With Tim and Bob, circa 1931

Also to earn some pocket money, Bob and I also started selling the *Saturday Evening Post* and *Ladies Home Journal* magazines. When dad saw our interest making money, he went to the auction market and bought Bob and I used bicycles. Dad thought, "Gosh, a used one is just as good as a new one." The new ones were maybe fifteen or twenty dollars, and these were three dollars and a half. It didn't matter to us. This was a big occasion, getting our first bicycles.

Now, of course, since we had bikes, Dad said we had to get a paper route. He wanted us to learn how to handle money. Bob and I delivered papers every day of the week, rain or shine, and we got a lot of rain in Albany! My mother made us additional rain clothes out of oilskin. Every afternoon after school, we would gather with the other paper boys to roll the papers and stuff them into our canvas bags, which hung on the bikes' handlebars. We'd pack enough newspapers to cover the customers on our assigned routes and off we rode every afternoon except on Sunday. On that morning, we had to get the thicker Sunday editions out before six a.m. It was usually still dark when we pedaled over to where the guys on a truck would dump off a pile of city newspapers from Portland.

After preparing the papers, Bob rode off to throw them onto the porches of his customers, and I rode off to do the same for mine. I had about forty-five customers in my designated area, which was downtown. My route was easier than Bob's for delivery purposes, but harder when it came to collecting at the end of the month. At each month's end, keeping track of who owed what, I had to knock on my customers' doors and collect the money for the papers, even as a little boy. Once in a while, somebody decided not to pay or just put me off or didn't answer the door. I'd have to try again another day or have to swallow the cost. It was terrible! Luckily, it didn't happen very often, and it wasn't hard to ask people for the money they owed. They understood what we were doing, collecting the fifty cents a month they owed for their paper delivery. Bob and I made ten or fifteen dollars a month and thought we were rich.

More Fun in Albany

Once we had bikes, we could roam farther in Albany. Sometimes we'd ride them into the main part of town and go to Owl Drug Store to the soda fountain. We also liked to ride to the bridge to watch the log trucks. After returning from the forest, they would stop their trucks on the logging road by a bank about 100 feet above the river and roll the logs down to the river where the timber would crash down the slope and splash dramatically into the water before making their way down current to the mills. It was pretty sensational for little kids to watch.

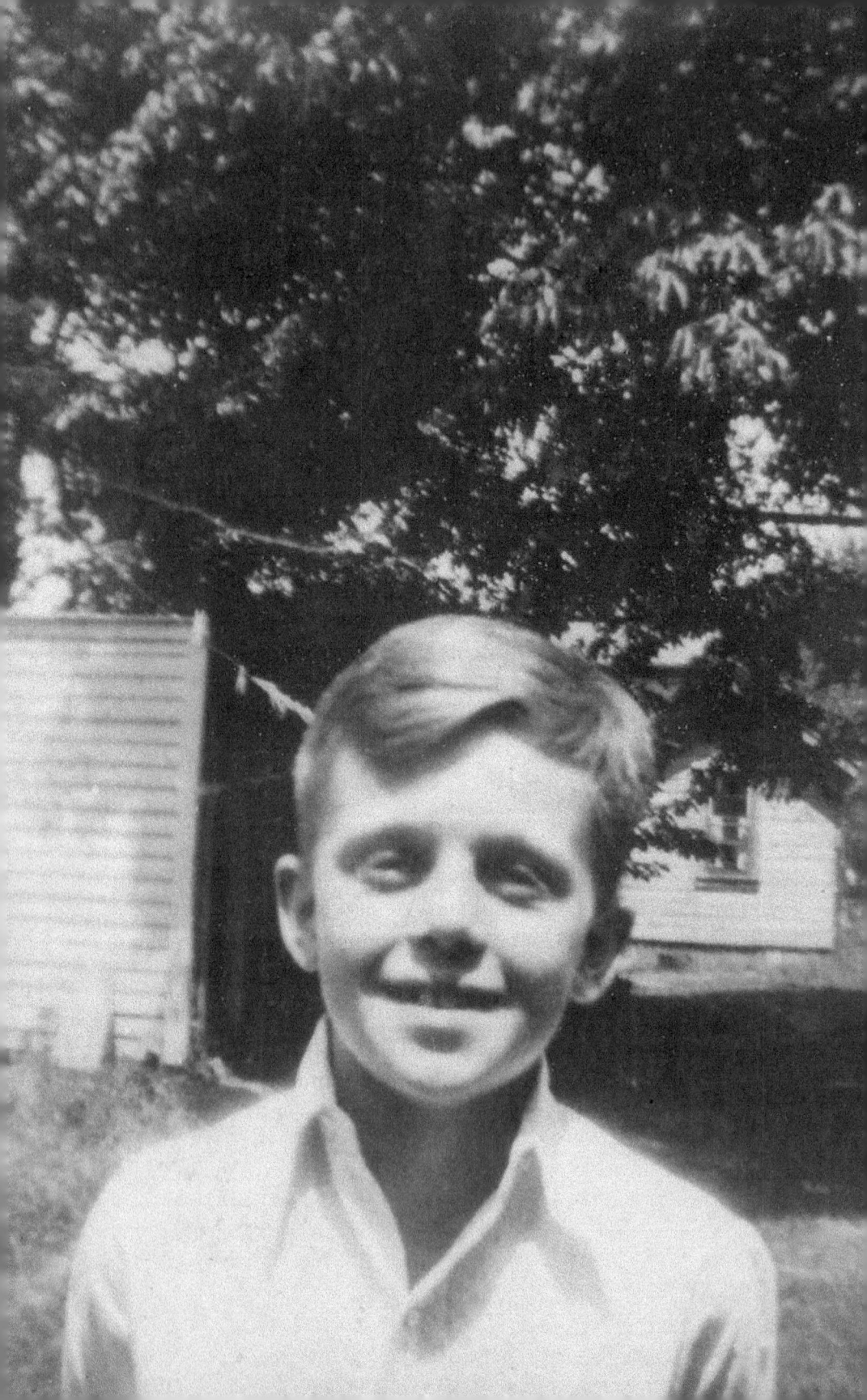

Chapter Two

Junior High at Central 1936 to 1938

SOON ENOUGH, WE WERE ENTERING CENTRAL JUNIOR HIGH SCHOOL, which then included seventh, eighth, and ninth grades. Our first year took place in the original building, an old wooden structure with a big tower where it had been for a long time. But my second year, we moved into a new, nice brick building, and the old one was torn down. We had to walk a little farther to school at 336 SW 9th Avenue, but that was fine. I was still just 11 years old, turning 12 during the school year, and yet like the rest of the boys, I was starting to feel my oats. My seventh-grade teacher, Bess Gieble was very pretty with a lovely figure. I knew I was not supposed to be looking at that sort of thing, but I was a growing, pubescent boy. We guys were all convinced that this one older boy in school, who acted older and was more physically mature, was seeing her on the side.

Mother always encouraged us to get good grades and study. We resisted her efforts at this rambunctious age, and when the teachers would tell her that we could and should do better, Bob replied that "average was good enough." I made myself do okay.

Just like in elementary school, I felt that studying and learning, why that was just what you did, but I liked the social part of junior high school. So did Bob.

School Boy Patrol

They had a duty at Central called the School Boy Patrol. If somebody was late to class or a parent was coming into school, you would escort them or tell them where to go. It wasn't much, just patrolling in front of the school. Most of the real guys didn't go in for that, but my brother and I volunteered. It was social and something to do.

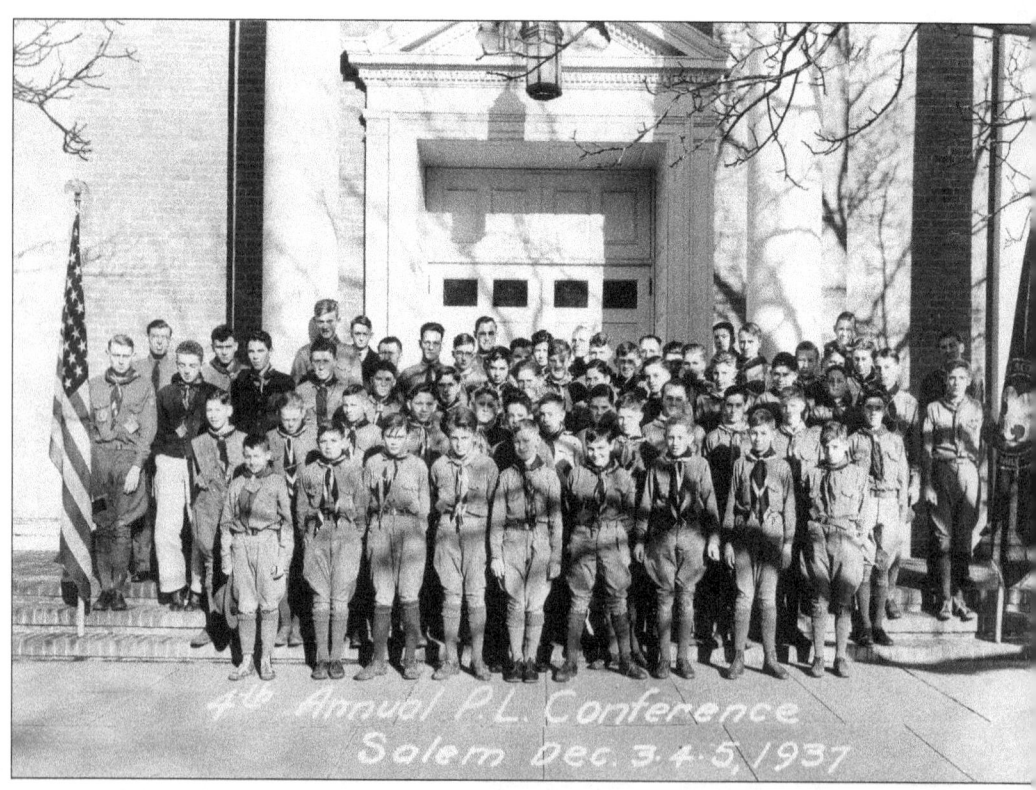

I'm in the third row, sixth from the right.

A Tenderfoot Going for Eagle

Both Bob and I were very involved in scouting during our junior high years. I wanted to be a Tenderfoot and work my way to Eagle Scout. In order to achieve Tenderfoot, I had to present myself as a leader, prepare for and take an overnight camping trip, and earn a number of merit badges, which demonstrated I knew how to tie certain knots, apply first aid, identify hazardous plants, keep physically fit, and other scouting skills. I joined local Panther Troop 10 and made Tenderfoot on June 3, 1936, then second class, first class and finally Star on October 14, 1937. By then I was the Panther Patrol Leader, had six merit badges, attended camporee and the Patrol Leaders Conference, and hiked Snow Peak at 4,183 feet, 30 miles east of Albany. I had a full uniform and my nickname was German.

My old camping journal lists a few of my favorites in 1937:

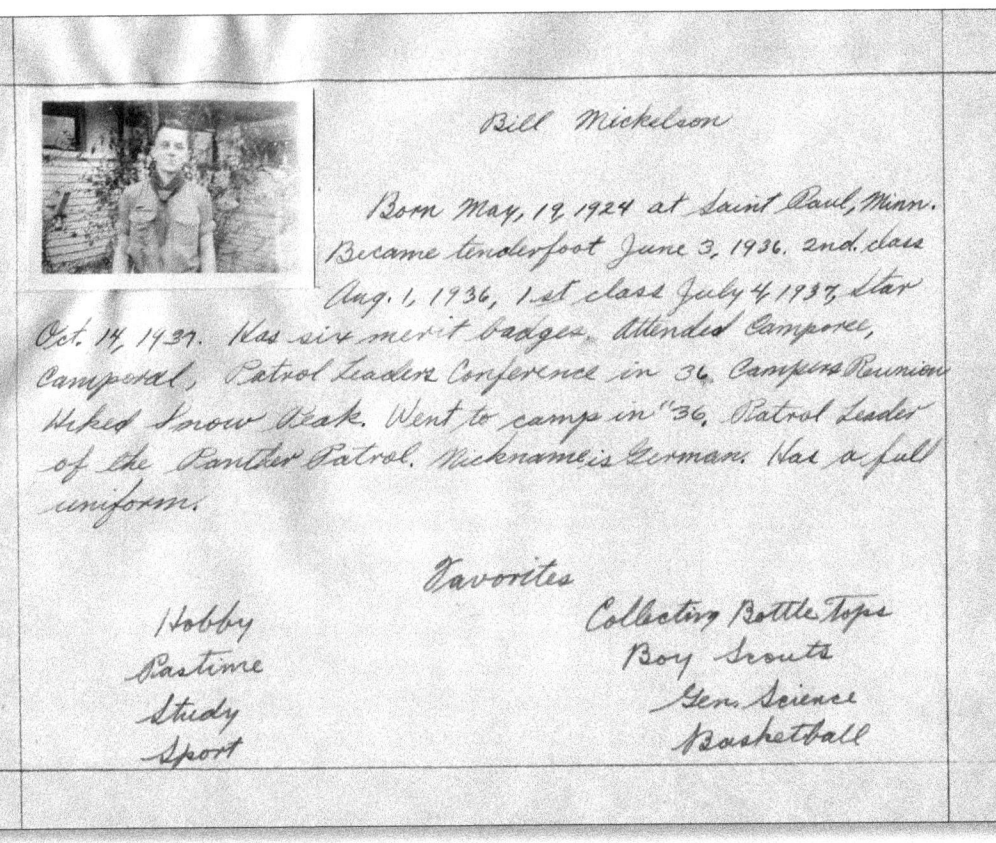

On the Peak of Mount Washington

A real highlight of my scouting days was at 12 years old when I was eligible to go to Camp Pioneer Boy Scout summer camp. The most talked about experience at Pioneer was climbing Mount Washington, not too far from Black Butte. We stood at the foot of the mountain, looking ahead at the glacial snow on the cornice, then off we went. A trail takes you towards the peak, over 10,000 feet above sea level. Up we climbed. The tricky part was the final spire, 200 feet, straight up and narrow. I don't know how we did it when we were twelve and thirteen or why my mother would even let me go! Actually, she didn't know that I was going to climb it. As far as she knew, I was just going to camp out. But we made it to the peak, a rocky plateau only about 12 x 12. Rocks took you just a little higher to the very top, but the area was so small, you had to hug the boulders between your knees to stay on it securely. There was a hiking log book up there in which you could sign your name and the date. I didn't want to let go of the top of the mountain to sign the log. Chattering and shivering, I finally grabbed the log book with my teeth, hugged the rock between my knees tightly and signed it. Then, I looked up. I could see for forty miles. I could see the curve of the earth. Even though I was with others, it felt like it was just me and the mountain and the world below. It was quite a triumph really, especially at that age.

Coming down, we had the fun of running down the snow field. It was pretty steep. We'd jump, throwing our feet out from under us and slide in the snow and then jump again back to tree level.

I took my son Mike up there when he was fifteen or sixteen on a trip arranged by our friend, Maynard Chambers. He climbed it just like I did. There were six of us hiking that day, first the gradual uphill, then the technical climb to the peak. There we were, together, sitting on the top looking out into the distance, just like I had at twelve.

But getting ready to go down, we looked at that 200-foot drop, and nobody wanted to take the lead. Though the route down was not completely vertical, it was still scary. You couldn't see where you were stepping, and you'd better step right. We weren't tied together. We had no safety ropes or anything, just one regular rope that whoever went first had to find a path for the rest of us and repel down. It was difficult and scary and a misstep could mean a drop. I didn't volunteer. One young man was going to go down first, but he just shivered and shook and then froze. We untied the rope on him. My son, bless his heart, volunteered. I've always been proud of him for that. He led the descent and made it, of course, leading the rest of us down safely, as just a teenager. The snow was melted, but just like we did as kids down the snow field, Mike and the others ran down and jumped ran the scree field laughing most of the way.

To Be an Eagle, You've Got to Swim

I had tackled Mount Washington, and yet I was still one badge from achieving Eagle Scout, because I couldn't swim. We lived close to what we called a lake too, Little Ditch, only two blocks away on 8th Street. It was a drain off of the Big Ditch and served as the town's swimming hole. We'd wade around in the shallows and play and tease each other and splash the girls and throw rocks. The bottom was smooth, not too deep. I think it even had boards laid on the bottom in some places and a little roof built over a portion of it to block the sun. But in order to go Eagle, I had to swim in deep waters.

The scouts, Billy and Bobby, 1937

I remember at least one circumstance during my elementary school years when two kids who knew how to swim said, "Let's go swimming in the lake!" And I said, "Okay, let's go!" I really wasn't afraid of the water then, and I was with three or four other boys who could swim, so I thought to myself, "I can swim, too. Nothing to it!"

But I couldn't. There was a short segment of a log in the water, and I grabbed on to that for dear life. Then they kicked it away from me, and I flailed about in the water. I don't know why I didn't drown that day. You never forget the day when you almost drown!

Finally, when I turned fourteen, my mom got us Red Cross swimming lessons taught by Harry Harvey in Bryant Park in the Willamette River. It took place in June when the water was freezing, and both Bob and I were more than a little afraid of the water with years of anticipation and not knowing how, and that near drowning day, as I remembered it. The first lessons in that cold water were rather torturous, but we did learn. Unfortunately, by then we were no longer in the scouts, so I never made Eagle. That was a little disappointing.

Sons of American Legion

Bob and I were members of the Sons of the American Legion. The American Legion, a veteran group supporting other veterans, was chartered by congress in 1919 and was pretty prominent right after World War I, and Dad was very active in the organization. The first convention convened in Minneapolis while my dad still lived there. Today, the American Legion is the largest wartime veterans service organization. In Albany, they were the fellows he played baseball with, and they all shared those horrible memories of the trenches, even if they didn't speak of them.

Uncle Jack, Bob and me doing some fishing, circa 1936

The Sons of the American Legion, formed in 1932 in Portland, Orgeon, was made up of male descendants of people who served in the United States Armed Forces during wartime. It reached a peak in 1939. My dad and a group of veterans wanted the Legion to persevere, so they organized the Sons of Legion in our town for us kids, but I don't remember much in the way of activities other than the dads saying, "You kids meet over there, and we're going to meet here." However, Dad was one of the founders of the American Legion Junior baseball program in 1940, and of course, Bob and I played in the league.

Still Tall Enough for Basketball

Church activities and Sunday school become more interesting in those early junior high years, but not so much for the worship, but because of the basketball team and the Sunday Youth programs. We found ourselves playing ball and hanging out with a large group of boys our age, all leaders at school like us, the Ralston boys, the Swansons, the Millers, the Obersons, and others. Of course, this brought a number of those "dumb" girls that we didn't really appreciate…not yet.

Work at the Butcher Shop Increases

By the time I was twelve, my work load had increased in the butcher shop. One of my new steady jobs was skinning calves. Two or three times a week, the farmers would bring in two to four all gutted, some with the head on, and we'd hang them up on a rail. First, I had to remove the hides. I had to sever the legs with a really sharp knife, splitting each to take the skin all the way down. I got so I could skin left-handed and upside down, pulling down the hide with my right hand from the body, neck and legs. To make it more enjoyable I timed myself. The fastest I ever skinned a calf was seven minutes. That's pretty fast! It was good for me, I guess. I grew up tough, and I learned to work and developed a skill.

When I grew a little older, I'd prepare the hogs we bought from the farmers too. The farmer would kill each hog and put it in severely hot water to take all the hair off the skin, and then let it cool. The lard left in its thick skin was about an inch thick all over. First, I had to take the head off of each pig. My dad's farmer friend, Ed Dayerty would come in during the morning and help me. When I first started as a scrawny twelve-year-old, barely big enough to get up to the block and sever the meat off the head, Ed did much of the work. But it wasn't long before I was doing most of the process myself.

With Dad, dressed for work at Harry's Market, circa 1937

After cutting off the head, we'd bone it, getting all the meat out, about a half a pound to a pound of meat out of every head. We'd sharpen our knives, and I learned how to slice out all the meat properly. Pigs' cheeks are a delicacy, very delicious. Then there's the rest of meat, behind the ears and the eyes. I must have taken the meat out of thousands of pigs' heads during the two decades-plus I worked in Pfeiffer's and Harry's Market.

Ed Dayerty and I would talk as we worked. He'd tell me his philosophy of life, which included what to do to get the girls to come around and how to keep them coming around. He said I should always keep myself clean and presentable. He always kept himself and his car very clean. He was about forty, old from my point of view, and made his money by playing the stock market, enough to have his own car. Every day, after we got through with the pigs' heads and everything was cleaned up, he'd sit in his car reading the stock exchange page of the newspaper to figure out his next move. We didn't pay him anything for his work each morning at Harry's Market. I think he just wanted something hands-on to do.

Another of my jobs starting when I was 12 was to carry quarters of beef into the walk-in cooler. They weighed 160 pounds. I weighed about 105. There were usually two of us in the back who handled the meat, and my brother and another guy waited on customers, along with my dad.

A Mikkelson Christmas

Christmas was always wonderful in our house, a big deal. My mother transferred the Christmas tradition from her upbringing to our family. Of course, there was extra work at the meat market beforehand to make sure everyone had their Christmas roasts and turkeys. But the arrival of the our tree and presents, visiting relatives, songs at the piano, and celebrations at church were worthwhile rewards.

The year we received our tricycles stands out in my memory. Neighbor kids had them, and we didn't, and we complained to our mother. We wouldn't dream of complaining to our dad! Seeing them beside the tree was very exciting.

In probably ninth grade, our parents gave us new bikes with balloon tires to replace the used ones. This made the delivery of papers much easier, and we felt pretty big for our britches as we rode those bikes with wide-Western handlebars that allowed us to give rides to other guys or maybe even a girl on the handlebars or crossbar. The bikes could be steered without hands too.

Though Dad's brother, Uncle Roy, wasn't much of a worker, he was a great gift giver. He had no children of his own and tried to give us something special for Christmas. One year, his gift was a real Daisy BB gun for each of us. He told us that someday he would give us each a .22, but I think Mom got in the way of that promise. We would practice hitting cherries placed on the wooden backyard fence, making quite a stained mess after several days of target practice.

A New Radio

Business at Harry's Market got better as the effects of the Great Depression lessened and the war started in Europe. We could afford to buy a stand-up radio. It was a beautiful piece of furniture in a big wood box. We'd sit on the floor and nuzzle up to the radio and listen to One Man's Family. That was a treat, although we weren't allowed too much time to do that. Most of the time we were playing outdoors or working, mowing lawns, delivering papers, and more and more, working at the market. This continued into our high school years.

Happy with our Daisy BB guns and pilot uniforms, with Uncle Roy, 1936

Chapter Three

High School Years 1938 to 1941

ALBANY HIGH WAS A SENIOR HIGH SCHOOL spanning three years, sophomore to senior year and overall, I had a great experience. Of course, Bob and I worked in the butcher shop pretty much every day after school and on Saturdays. It was quite known that we could be found there when not playing sports or at school or church activities, so much so that our quote for our Senior Will in the yearbook was, "We, Bill and Bob Mikkelson, will be happy to serve you. Thank you."

Harry's Market Every Day

I weighed probably 135 throughout most of high school and still only weighed about 150 pounds by the time I was a senior at seventeen years old, but I was used to carrying those quarters of beef into the cooler to hang them on hooks. As I got older, the beef got heavier, up to 200 pounds, so I learned to be strong despite my size.

With a steady flow of business, my dad hired a couple fellows, Orville Steeprow and Alvin Little, to work in the shop, along with me, Bob, Ed, and my mom. Like Ed, these fellows would give me advice once in a while about life. They didn't have big careers or anything, but they were older than me. Most of the advice was about girls.

Bashful Billy & Girls

Now, when it came to girls, Bob just seemed to know what to do. He knew how to handle them. He dated all the time. The girls couldn't leave him alone. He was labeled in our senior yearbook as the "Worst Ladies' Man," meaning he was good with the gals. We were the same height, but we didn't even look like brothers by then. He was always a charming and very good-looking guy. He understood about fashion. During our high school days, boys wore tan-colored corduroy pants, and you weren't supposed to not wash them so they'd get stiff. I'd get ready to fold them to put them in a drawer, and Bob would say, "No, stand them up!"

Working at Harry's, 1939. I'm third from left. Bob is second from right. Dad stands between us.

He shared that with me but not his skill with the ladies! In contrast, I didn't know how to be around girls. Every time I saw a pretty girl, I just withered.

One of the prettiest girls in my grade when I was fourteen and fifteen was Billie Fitzpatrick. She would come in and see me once in a while in the meat market. But I was so bashful, I didn't know what to do. The guys in the shop would feed me lines and tell me how to treat her. Finally, Ed said, "Why don't you take her out?

Handsome Brother Bob's senior portrait

"Well, it would cost me seventy-five cents," I replied, thinking of a place like the Elite Cafeteria, the local soda fountain. It was a big place with a counter where kids often hung out and ate. But really, I was just too scared to ask.

We finally had one "date" that was hardly a date. We rode bicycles and just sat and talked. I don't remember ever spending any money on Billie, having a Coca-Cola together or anything, and I certainly never hugged or kissed her. As I recall, we only had the one outing together, but it was fairly significant to me since she was the first girl I tried to spend time with. Otherwise, I didn't have any girlfriends in high school, not until I met Fern. They were too scary. If they talked to me, walking by in the hallway at school, I put my head down.

Despite my awkwardness, the beautiful Marky Weatherford was nice to me. One year, there weren't enough lockers to go around, so we all had to partner up, and the popular and pretty Marky invited me to share her locker. Weatherford was a very famous and important name in Oregon. William Washington Weatherford was an Oregon pioneer who traveled the original 2,200-mile Oregon Trail from Missouri and helped establish the new territory.

His grandson, Marion T. Weatherford, founded the Oregon Wheat Commission, the first of its kind in the nation. James Knox Weatherford, Sr., Marky's grandfather (1850–1935) served as the Oregon Speaker of the House followed by three terms in the state senate, and Marky's father was a respected agricultural consultant for the governor. I was younger than Marky. All the girls were older than me in my class since I had skipped a grade. But she never teased me or made me feel inferior. I always liked her for that.

A Bulldog in High School Sports

I continued my habit in high school, being a year younger than everyone in my class, of trying to play harder and better than the rest in order to keep up and make my mark. Our school mascot was the Bulldog, and I guess you could say that suited me. Despite my bashfulness, I was pretty involved at school, taking on quite a few positions of leadership.

Bob and I were both lettermen and wore our yellow

Playing for the Bulldogs, circa 1940

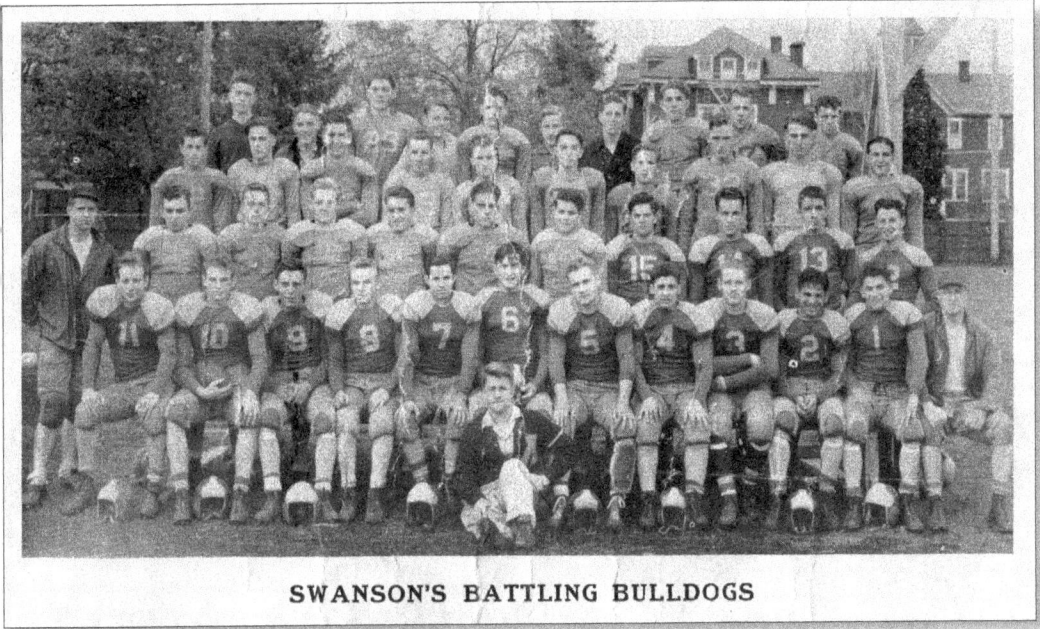

SWANSON'S BATTLING BULLDOGS

I'm second row, second player from left.

stripes on our jackets to signify this. The first two years, I played basketball and football on Coach Swanson's Battling Bulldogs. I played all three years of varsity baseball. That was my main sport. In addition, I was in the Archery Club for two years and boxed my sophomore year.

A Small Tight End

In football, I played tight end mostly, despite my small size. My competition for the position, the starting tight end on our team, was big and tough and his dad had been a star college football player, so I didn't get to play very much. I usually sat on the bench. I loved to practice though and loved to hit. I tackled hard and could bring down somebody that weighed 200 pounds, just like the sides of meat I carried in the shop. I'd just tackle the guy as hard as I could. I worked really hard at football. As a result, I got to play once in a while. When we were ahead.

A 'Short' Career in Basketball

Bob and I started playing basketball on community teams when we were little, and I always enjoyed the sport. But as other guys grew past me in height, I became just too tiny to compete. The high school coach even asked me to quit the team because I was too short, though he didn't say it that way. Maybe this shows my personality a little. I pretended like I didn't hear him, and I showed up the next day. Finally, I got embarrassed and left. That was the end of basketball for me, except for some lowkey city league play in adulthood.

In the Ring

During the one year that I boxed for the Albany Bulldogs, I was also fighting in the community ring on occasion. One time in our community gym, I was set to box an opponent from Lebanon, Oregon. Though he was in my weight range, he turned out to be eighteen. I was only fifteen. That wasn't too good a deal! But of course, I thought I could take him anyway. I'd been boxing a long time. But I learned that day that I hadn't been slugging it out like the older guys. When you're twelve and thirteen, you don't fight the same as when you're sixteen or seventeen.

At the bell, we went in fighting, and it wasn't long before he knocked me out cold. I lay on the mat flat on my back not knowing what was going on, no idea. Neither my mother or father was there, but my preacher, Daniel Poling, was, a very famous guy in our town by then. He hurried to the ring and stopped the match.

"We're not going to have this anymore. I'm taking this boy," he said. With some help, he carried me unconscious back home where he slapped my face and sprayed cold water on it until I woke up.

That guy from Lebanon was really a boxer. I thought I was, but he was greater, and being eighteen made a big difference, not just in size but understanding how to fight.

Bulldog Baseball

As a result of all the flyballs Dad hit to us, I got to be a pretty good fielder and was a strong hitter. Bob and I and the Bulldog team even won the coast championship during high school.

It also helped that Bob and I went to baseball camp while in high school. My mother wanted us to be busy during the summer, so she signed us up for Carl Mays' baseball school in Salem, Oregon, two different summers. Mays was a pitcher for the Yankees and played with Babe Ruth. He was also the first submarine pitcher in the major leagues. In the submarine motion, the pitcher releases the ball in a kind of twisting side arm close to the ground. A right-hander, Mays won over 200 games, 27 in 1921 alone, and was a member of three world championship teams. We drove twenty miles to Salem five days a week, played a ton of ball

Playing for the Bulldogs, circa 1940

and got instruction from Mays for most of the summer. I think my mother paid $200 a piece for that school, which was a lot of money. There were maybe twenty-five kids in the class. It was big time, working with a pro. He taught everything about baseball: stealing bases, catching flies, getting a start while running, so we got to be pretty good.

I usually played first base and was the cleanup hitter quite often. I'd hit home runs and steal bases when I could. It was exciting.

My good friend in Albany, Bud Fortier, was a few years younger than us. We played together for the city league. Like our dad, his dad, Al Fortier, took him out every Sunday, showing him how to throw a curveball and pitch consistent fast balls. Besides pitching, Bud could play any position and often played shortstop when he wasn't on the mound. His dad coached the championship 1942 and 1943 Bulldogs (for which Bud played) after our coach Dwight Adams was conscripted into the military in the summer of 1941, which was also just after Bob and I graduated. Bud was good enough to play professionally and was drafted by the San Francisco Seals of the Pacific Coast League in 1947.

In my Albany city league uniform

Catching a pop-up at first for the Bulldogs, 1940

He came home with a great big signing bonus, $20,000, which was a lot of money in those days. Of course, now they give players two million dollars. He also came home in a shiny white car with a rumble seat and white sidewalls. If I recall correctly, I bought that car from him eventually. Bud went on to play for the Yakima Bears in the Western International League. During the writing of this book, he was still living in Albany and we're still good friends.

High School Clubs Galore

You could say I was a joiner. Because I competed in intramural sports, I was in the school's sports club called the Associated Bulldogs all three years, serving as leader of the club my junior year. During my senior year, I was in the Order of A (a club made up of boys who have earned letters in any of the four major sports, football, basketball, track, and baseball), and the Boys Athletic Association (B.A.A.).

I was in Hi-Y junior and senior years. Hi-Y was affiliated with the Young Men's Christian Association (YMCA). The purpose of it and the girls' club, Tri-Hi-Y was "to create, maintain and extend, throughout the home, school, and community, high standards of Christian character." During my senior year, the club held a Mothers' Day breakfast, our annual picnic, visited other Hi-Y chapters, sold hot dogs and ice cream at football and basketball games, handled fire drills and policed the annual carnival parade. We contributed to a couple school funds and prizes and received high acclaim for exemplary church attendance. I served as the school Chaplain my junior year.

Circa 1939

I joined Quill and Scroll (an international high school journalism honor society), which met the first Monday of each month for a dinner and business meeting, because during my sophomore year, I became the sports writer for our school newspaper, *The Whirlwind*. I reported on the scores and gameplay of the various sports teams on campus. This started my "sports journalism career."

Circa 1938

A Fifteen-Year Old Newspaper Man

One day, I was in the alley behind the butcher shop. The office for the town's local newspaper, the *Albany Democrat Herald* was right across the alley. You could hear the typeset printers in the basement working away, whirring and clicking out the papers. The guy who managed the paper, Walter, happened to come out at the same time and saw me.

"You're writing sports for *The Whirlwind*, aren't you?"

I told him I was. He told me their sports editor Andy Dooley had quit and asked me if I would work for him. I didn't hesitate to say yes.

I turned out two or three stories each week for the Democrat, covering Albany's semi-pro baseball team and the Albany high school football and baseball teams. I didn't have anything to do with basketball as a journalist. Being only fifteen, I couldn't drive when I first started the job. When I could drive and got a car, I occasionally attended games out of town (sometimes I was playing in them!)

Writing for the city paper really taught me how to write. People at the newspaper showed me how to set up each article with the title and the subhead and paragraphs and edited my pieces. I even learned how to typeset it, and after that always typeset my own articles for printing. The work earned me five dollars a week. That was more than mowing lawns!

I was pretty darn proud of the fact that I had stories in the paper, even though I couldn't put my name on the articles, being a staff reporter. When each paper came out, my mother cut out the pieces I wrote and saved them in a scrapbook.

It was funny when I had to cover a game in which I was playing. One time, our high school varsity baseball team was playing our arch rivals from Corvallis for the district championship, and I hit the homerun that won the ball game. Well, I had to include that in the story, so I wrote about myself in third person, describing the home run. "The batter, Bill Mikkelson, hit the ball way over the left field fence."

When I came into the office the next day, Walter saw me and grinned, "Oh, I see where you hit the ball way over the fence." We both laughed.

> **Albany Trips Lebanon, 6-5**
>
> ALBANY, May 15 (Special) Bill Mikkelson, Albany high school outfielder and first baseman, became the hero of a ten-inning baseball game here Tuesday night when he poked a bunt just inches inside first base line for a single that brought in the winning run of a 6-5 victory for the Bulldogs over the Lebanon Berrypickers.
>
> The loss dropped Lebanon into a tie with Sweet Home for first place in the northern division of district No. 7.
>
> Score:
> Lebanon ---- R H E / 5 3 4
> Albany ---- 6 4 3
> Ellis and Heidinger, Thoma; and Hermans. Kennel

I was still writing for the *Democrat Herald* after graduating from high school. In one of my articles, I announced that the Albany Alcos were going to play the team in Silverton at 2:30 in the afternoon in Silverton, which is fifteen miles out of town. Turns out there was no game. I had the day wrong! I made sure that didn't happen again.

The Prez

Participating and taking on roles in leadership were ways I tried to make my mark and stand equal to my older classmates. I served as class president both sophomore and junior years and student body president my senior year, while Bob became senior class president.

> **Bill Mikkelson Heads Albany High Students**
>
> Bill Mikkelson, son of Mr. and Mrs. Harry Mikkelson and a junior in Albany high, was recently elected student body president of Albany high school.
>
> The new student head has been active in extra-curricular programs during the past two year, heading the sophomore class in 1938-39 and the junior class this year, 1939-40. He is a member of the varsity football and baseball squads, also.
>
> Chosen vice-president was Norman Oberson, son of Mr. and Mrs. Henry L. Oberson. Patricia Stuart, daughter of Mr. and Mrs. J. L. Stuart, was named student secretary and Bobby Reid, son of Dr. and Mrs. G. F. Reid, was elected treasurer.
>
> Yell leaders elected for the coming year include Jerry Lee Miller, Shirley Pratt and Calvin Tigner.
>
> Mildred Marsh was named subscription manager of the Whirlwind, high school publication, and Phyllis Hancock was chosen business manager.

Our friend Richard Miller was running against me in the election for student body president and happened to be one of our star football players. His dad had been a star football player and so was his brother. (Richard went on to play college ball.) He was well known, well liked, good looking, and audacious. I thought, "Well, what the heck! I might as well try. I probably can't win against Richard. So, if he wins, he's supposed to win." With nothing to lose, I challenged him and, lo and behold, I was elected. That was pretty nice.

As class president, I had over 150 kids looking to me and as student body president, the entire school. The drive to make my mark may have been my initial motivation, but I also found pleasure in serving others, being charitable. I felt gratified for my actions, receiving both internal and external rewards. I found I truly liked to help other people, especially when I recognized their compassion and love. The value of service, first instilled in me by my mother and church and reinforced in high school, remained important to me my entire life.

I guess I achieved my goal of standing out. *The Whirlwind* Yearbook Senior Review, described me as "Personality Plus," and in senior voting, I was voted "Most Popular and Outstanding Boy." How about that?

The only thing I dreaded when I became Student Body President was getting up on stage and speaking to the entire school. I had a bit of stage fright. But I knew I had to get up there and speak. It was part of the job. As soon as I was elected, I enrolled in a speaking course in town that lasted most of the first semester of my senior year. The twenty-week class met once a week. Every other week, the twenty people in the class either wrote a speech or gave a speech. So, each session, ten people spoke. It was good training.

That Fabulous Hudson

Throughout my life, when I've seen opportunities poke their heads up, I've often grabbed them. As an example, when I was in high school very few people had cars in Albany, particularly youngsters. Well, for a couple weeks on my way to high school each day in 1940, I regularly passed by this car with a flat tire parked on the side of the street in front of a house. It was a gorgeous little car:

In my Hudson convertible, 1940

Flying High

The Hudson in front of our house

a yellow-cream-colored 1932 Hudson Terraplane convertible with white sidewalls and silver-wire wheels and a six-inch high shorty-windshield. It had an all-leather interior and leather rumble seat. It was a fast-looking car too. You just didn't see cars like that. And yet the Terraplane just sat there for weeks. I finally decided if it was just going to sit there, I wanted that car.

I went up and knocked on the front door. An acquaintance of mine answered, a fellow named Don, about my age.

"What about your car, Don?" I asked.

"Oh, do you want to buy it?"

"Yeah." I said, "How much do you want for it?"

"Well, how does eighteen dollars sound?"

I paid him, and the car was mine. Now here's the crazy part of the story. Two days later, Don came by and gave me a dollar back. He thought he charged me too much for it! Today, that car would be worth two-and-a-half million or more fixed up as a collector car.

I patched the tire and did a few other things to get it going. The engine ran just wonderfully; there was nothing wrong with it. We had a lot of fun with that car. Of course, the rumble seat was pretty important, a ride home for girls or stuffed full of guys from the baseball team. It was a fast car as well. We used to race it once in a while on country roads, and it would beat all the other cars.

One time, Bob asked me if he could drive the Hudson. Of course, I said yes. We had a friend with us, a big guy that weighed probably 250, and all three of us were in the front seat, which was built for two. The big guy was on the end. I don't remember exactly what caused Bob to do it, but he drove my car into the ditch on the side of the road, and we rolled on the soft top, perhaps with the weight of our friend pitching us just enough to roll over.

We did a quick inspection of ourselves and the car. I was in the middle and got cut and was bleeding. I still have the scar on my left upper arm. Bob and our friend were fine. The rear-view mirror broke, but otherwise, the roll didn't seem to do much damage. We just needed help to get the car out of there. I replaced the mirror and had the Terraplane back on the road in no time.

I've never been much of a car guy. I like planes. But that Hudson was a great first car, and it became essential later in my senior year when it allowed me to drive out to the farm to pick up Fern for dates.

Meeting Fern Morse

One of my best friends during our senior year started going steady with a gal who went to Corvallis High. Corvallis is about ten miles from Albany and was our main rival in high school sports. Her name was Dorothy Morse. I'm not sure how he met her, but that was a big deal, going steady. It meant you wouldn't date anybody else. I can't remember exactly what happened, if they broke up or she and

Fern and Dorothy Morse with their mother Emma, 1944

my friend were apart for a while, but I took Dorothy on one date. Maybe we went as friends. Well, because of my grade-skip, I was still just sixteen years old even though I was a senior, and Dorothy spent most of the evening telling me how to treat girls.

Fern when I met her at sixteen, 1941

She had a lot to say about how to act around girls and especially dress for girls, like to button my coat, silly things like that. She and her family were fairly new to the area, having been brought up in Montana and Spokane, Washington.

When I dropped her off at home, out on a farm halfway between Albany and Corvallis, she introduced me to her little sister, Fern. Both Morse sisters were very pretty, but Fern, a year behind me in school but the same age as me, sixteen, had a bright glow all about her and an infectious grin. She was a true beauty.

How lucky was I. Fern took a liking to me too and started "working on me." Soon after, her sister started dating the guy she would ultimately marry, and I asked Fern out on a date.

I couldn't get over how sweet Fern was. As we spent more and more time together, she made it easy for me to get over my shyness. Before too long, we were going steady. I'd go out often to see Fern at the farm. We'd go on dates, although it got so that just a telephone call, she would expect to get a date from me! But that was okay. We had a lot of fun. She taught me how to dance.

Falling in love with Fern, 1941

Because I hadn't dated, I didn't know how to dance until we started going out.

I got along well with her parents. They were good parents, a merry group. They tended to call me "Billy" and just welcomed me in. Her mother, Emma, was wonderful. Her daddy was a college man, a banker who thought he could be a farmer too. There weren't nearly as many men in his generation as there were in mine that went to college. He would often wear a vest and suit even around the house. He was a nice and placid person, very much a gentleman.

Fern's younger brother, Harold was known to everyone by his nickname, Putter. He was a short and strong guy, popular though he didn't go out with the girls. Her older brother, Lawrence, was away at college and eventually settled in Spokane, Washington.

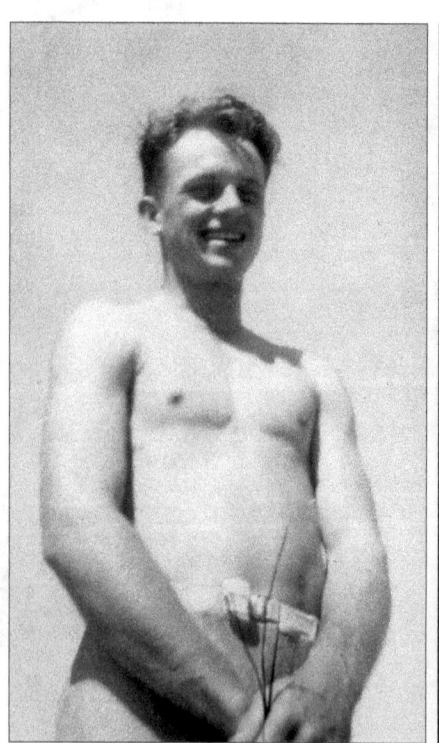 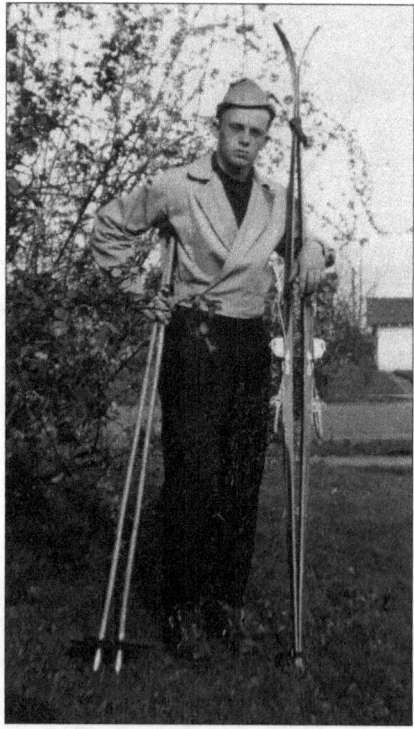

Other summer and winter fun during high school.

Graduation

I had just turned seventeen when I graduated from high school in June 1941 and was accepted to Oregon State University. Unlike the complicated process today, I filled out and mailed in my applications with my parents' permission and that was that.

High school graduation day for Bob and me, June 1941, with Fern and Shirley, our high school sweethearts and future wives

Dressed for the ceremony

How lucky were we to both get graduation kisses? A little lipstick still told the tale.

With Dad and Mom on graduation day, June 1941

Chapter Four

College Years
1941 to 1943

BOB AND I STARTED AT OREGON STATE TOGETHER. He was eighteen years old; I was seventeen. The Oregon State University campus is in Corvallis, a twenty-five-minute drive from home. There were many reasons to stay local. I had the Terraplane for the commute. Even though we were in college, we were still expected to help in Harry's Market, and Fern was in the picture, finishing her senior year at Corvallis High.

Choosing Chemical Engineering

I always had an interest in math and science, as a kid and in high school. But I didn't know what to choose for my major, so I asked Dan Poling Jr. Dan was on the faculty for Oregon State College at the time, but grew up in Albany. He went on to be known as "Dean Dan," remaining on the OSU faculty from 1937 to 1972 and serving as Dean of Men for many of those years. His father Daniel was not only our local pastor, he had directed the university's "Y-Hut," (The Y-Hut was removed in 1927 to make way for the Memorial Union), and Poling Hall, a residence hall, is named for him. The Polings were also neighbors of ours in Albany.

I asked Dan, "What's the toughest course you have at OSU?"

"Oh, chemical engineering," he replied.

I said, "I'll take it."

My parents thought that was nice, because I used to have a chemistry set growing up.

I had my first car, my first girlfriend, and I took nineteen hours of chemical engineering, wanting to conquer it, because it was the hardest course, still the Bulldog!

Becoming a Sigma Nu

I didn't do badly, making the honor roll the first year. That was important, not just for my own expectations but also you needed good grades to pledge a fraternity, and I wanted to pledge Sigma Nu. Bob didn't make his grades that first semester, taking general science. I wasn't smarter. I was just used to having to work harder and do what it takes to excel beyond people older and bigger than me. So, with my college courses and grades, I whacked it.

Daddy said, "I don't think you should join that fraternity until your brother can get in." But I pledged anyway.

Hazing was part of the initiation back then. The actives took us

Oregon State Sigma Nu house (I'm fifth from right first row), 1941

College Years

Dressed for a Sigma Nu theme party. I'm fifth from the right, 1941

down to the river in the dark and took our clothes away. It was so cold, while they slapped a rubber belt against our bare bottoms.

It was worth it. I have good memories of that time, the camaraderie and fun with my Sigma Nu brothers. We had dinner together every evening at the house, except the night the cook was off, and then a bunch of us went out to eat together. We had a choral group with 17 guys, and we won the interfraternity campus singing competition twice. There was always an intramural sports activity going on. With my Sigma Nu brothers, I played basketball, baseball, and ran cross country. All the while, I studied hard to keep up my grades and went on lots of dates with Fern.

Meat Instead of Roses

Freshman year, I lived in the fraternity house, rooming with the star of the football team, Don Durdan. He kind of watched over me. He'd say, "You'd better behave now."

Flying High

Studying, 1942

I worshipped him. Don was one of five guys in Sigma Nu on that year's champion football team that made it into the Rose Bowl.

By then, January 1st, 1942, we were at war. It was less than a month since the bombing of Pearl Harbor, and due to fears of an attack on the west coast by the Japanese, the Rose Bowl was held in Durham, North Carolina, instead of its usual location in Pasadena, California.

My brother and I would have loved to have gone to Durham to watch the game, but we didn't get to go, because my daddy wanted us in Albany to work in the butcher shop. Saturday was the busiest day of the week. So, instead of road-tripping with our buddies to watch our championship football team, we did what we always did on Saturdays, kill chickens, wait on customers, handle and cut meat, everything needed to run Harry's Market.

Oregon State won that Rose Bowl, 20 to 16 against the Duke Blue Devils. It was their only Rose Bowl win in history, and they've only been to the Rose Bowl three times. Don was named MVP (the only player from OSU ever inducted into the Rose Bowl Hall of Fame). It was a hard game to miss!

I finally went to watch Oregon State play in a Rose Bowl in 1956 in Pasadena, long after I was married and had kids. They lost to the Iowa Hawkeyes that year.

Don was conscripted into the Navy at the end of that year. After the war, he signed with the San Francisco 49ers for the 1946-47 seasons. During those same years, he played professional basketball for the Portland Indians of the Pacific Coast Professional Basketball League. The league folded in 1948. Don married a Corvallis girl, Maxine DeMoss, and took over her family's funeral home business. Sadly, he died when he was only 51 years old.

Baseball in College

Bob and I both played baseball for Oregon State. We had a great pitcher that first year, 1942, Herbert Glenn Elliott, a left-hander. After the war, he made it to the majors, pitching for the Boston Braves from 1947 to 1949. Sophomore year, however, I just enjoyed intramural sports.

During college, we also played once in a while for the Albany city team.

Ready to Go to War

When the Japanese bombed Pearl Harbor on Sunday morning December 7th, 1941, I didn't expect it. I think few Americans did. It was a busy time for me in college, but I read about it in the newspaper in shock, thinking how terrible it was and, of course, followed the news as we moved into World War II. We all had to register for the military and those over 20 years old were immediately conscripted into service. I wanted to apply, but I wasn't old enough. College boys like me went ROTC, and Bob and I were both issued military uniforms. Since I was majoring in engineering, I was put into the artillery, as all engineering students were. Bob, as a secretarial science major was put into the infantry. We took the training in ROTC seriously. Unless the war ended, it would just be a matter of time before we were in the fight.

Yours Truly, ROTC, 1942

Living in the Firehouse

My sophomore year, I made a mistake concerning my housing. Dorothy Morse was married by then and her husband Jake Prince worked for the Corvallis Fire Department. He said, "You know, you can move into the fire hall as a volunteer, and it won't cost you anything."

Well, it wouldn't have cost me anything anyway, because my dad was paying for college (He still didn't pay Bob and me to work at the meat market), but nevertheless, when Jake said that I thought, "Oh, that's a good deal."

I moved out of Sigma Nu and down to the fire hall. It was a dumb thing to do, one of the biggest mistakes of my life. You didn't have to pay money to stay there, but you did have to train and act as part of the volunteer fire department, which sometimes received a significant amount of emergency calls.

My first night there, the alarm went off. Before going to bed, we had to set up our pants hanging on our boots so we could dress quickly, slide down the fire pole just a few feet away, get on the truck and go. Well, I couldn't get my pants up. When I finally did, I looked down the pole, and the trucks were on their way out. I missed them.

It turned out not to matter. We had three fire alarms that first morning!

I made the second one and rode on the back of the fire truck, but I didn't have time to put my shirt on. It was about thirty degrees out. I was freezing as I helped feed the hose in and put the fire out.

Back at the firehouse, I had just gone back to sleep when the alarm shrieked again and off we went in the dark.

It was terrible! Most of all, I missed the fraternal relationships forged by living at Sigma Nu. Looking back, I can't think of anything good about living in the fire hall except it forced me to jump out of two-story windows, so I got pretty good at jumping a long way down onto a catch net.

If you're going to be a fireman, you've got to do things like that. I can still feel myself standing on the ledge of a two-story building and throwing my feet into the air, hoping that the fellows below caught me.

With an occasional lack of sleep, I still had to stay on top of my studies, and had I been in the fraternity, I could have gotten help on things. Maybe that's when I learned how to take power naps. But, I did save probably fifty dollars a month.

Falling Deeper in Love with Fern

Fern attending Oregon State, 1942

Fern and I saw each other whenever we could, even more so my sophomore year since she started at OSC that fall. Like her sister Dorothy, she joined Kappa Kappa Gamma sorority. I kept a little red book in my pocket in 1942 and '43, a daily journal. I tended to keep diaries most of my life, more so after reporting became a daily habit as Sports Editor of the Democrat Herald. In them, I would write briefly of the day's activities. In the little red book, Fern is mentioned in almost every entry. On a day we couldn't spend time together, I still wrote, "Didn't see Fern."

In a typical week, we might talk on the front steps of the firehouse or Kappa house on a Tuesday, meet up to talk in the park after a football game on Wednesday, go to a house dance on Saturday, and sit and talk or go to a movie Sunday evening after a full day of studying.

We had a "perfect time," I reported, at the sophomore cotillion in 1942, themed a Rio Rendezvous. "Fern was dressed in black and really looked swell. Serenaded afterward in the snow until 3:30 a.m. Dedicated one to Fern."

The next evening, I took her to the movies to see the *Black Swan* with Anthony Quinn and Tyrone Powers. Then we laid together in front of her fireplace at the Kappa house. It was wonderful having Fern in my life.

I continued to enjoy her family as well, and they seemed to like me. One fall, her dad wanted me to help out with the harvest on his farm. He paid me fifty cents an hour. That experience is on my "merit badge." I never ever worked on a farm again after that. It's just hot!

The War Calls

In November 1942, in the first semester of our sophomore year, the government lowered the age of men serving from 20 years old to eighteen. Bob and I were both old enough to be conscripted and go to war.

Bob, being ROTC infantry, received his orders right away. But I had signed up to be a Naval Aviation Cadet and go to flight school. Like any kid, I had always wanted to fly.

Fern at the Sigma Nu house, 1942

Dressed for a dance, 1942

In order to qualify for naval aviation, I had to complete two 4-month semesters (or 10-week "quarters") of college before attending pre-flight school. A good understanding of mathematics and science were considered essential. My job was to remain in school for the time being, though I was anxious to serve my country as many of us were at that time.

My parents and I worried about Bob being a soldier. We knew a lot of guys that went to Camp Adair, the base closest to home, right there in Corvallis, Oregon, including Fern's older brother Lorry. It was one of the biggest Army training bases on the west coast. Those fellows were there one day, you might even be going into town with them or something, and then they were shipped out the next. Sometimes you never saw them again. Most of them ended up in the infantry and on the front lines, and half the infantry was killed in battle in World War II. Seven out of ten suffered casualties. We lost a lot of our classmates.

Luckily, with his college experience, Bob was able to get assigned to an officers' school in Georgia and never had to go to the front. He stayed on the East Coast training others and escaped combat. We were all very happy about that.

Then there was me. With my college education, I was able to qualify for flight school, and the war ended before I could be deployed. I guess you could say college literally saved our lives. When the war ended, Mother had her two boys safe. But the family experienced a lot of anxiety for a few years. You never knew what might happen next during war time.

By June of 1943 at the end of my sophomore year at Oregon State, the U.S. had been at war for a year and a half. At nineteen years old, I was off to flight school on my way to becoming a fighter bomber pilot. That began an entirely new and exciting experience.

Bob (far left) and friends back for a break from basic training, 1943

Prepping meat for a beach barbecue while Bob and friends are on leave (Bob is standing to the right of me), 1943

Chapter Five

Military Years
1943 to 1945

I STARTED MY FLIGHT TRAINING IN MONMOUTH, ILLINOIS. It was the first of six different U.S. training bases where I spent time over the next two years. That included Beeville, Texas, the University of Georgia, which had been taken over in part by the military for training, Glenview Naval Air Station in Chicago, Illinois, Corpus Christi, Texas, and a final stint in Pensacola, Florida.

All during World War II, the U.S. Navy pilot training program had been ramping up. It had the same stages as the army aviation program (pre-flight, primary, basic, and advanced), except basic flight in the Navy added a carrier landing stage for fighter and torpedo- or dive-bomber pilots. I couldn't wait to get into a plane!

Saying good-bye to Fern and off to flight training, 1943

Naval Flight Preparatory School, Monmouth, Illinois

But I didn't see the inside of a cockpit for a while, not in flight preparatory school. Monmouth College was one of seventeen institutions selected by the U.S. Navy as a Naval Flight Preparatory School starting in January 1943. Many colleges were eager to host the military as a way to get by during the war with the lack of students. In 30 months, more than 4,000 Navy men went through Monmouth College, including me as part of the 10th Battalion.

Flight preparation at Monmouth College was mostly textbook work. Much of the classroom work was rooted in math and science, thus the importance of my college experience. A lot of theoretical knowledge was needed before a pilot could undertake the practicalities of combat flying. We took courses in physics, advanced mathematics, flight dynamics, weather, and basic mechanics. Some of the learning was broad: covering the science of aerodynamics and how to think in three dimensions. Some of it was more directly practical: the capabilities of the planes; angles of attack; the best positions from which to kill an enemy aircraft; and how to pull out of an impending crash.

I finished the coursework in late December 1943. It was useful, but I couldn't wait to actually fly!

Cubs & Perils, Beeville, Texas

At the Naval Air Station Chase Field at Beeville, Texas, we finally got into hands-on flight training. I was still just nineteen years old when I piloted an airplane for the first time. During our first flights, we were accompanied by instructors. We went up in these small piston-driven cubs that had canvas tops over the cockpits. The propellers had to be turned by hand to get them started. Such out-of-date planes weren't needed for warfare. After 20 hours of flight time if the instructor deemed you confident, you soloed.

Once we mastered the training planes in those cubs, we piloted

Yellow Perils, also known as the Naval Aircraft Factory N3N Canaries. The Peril was a biplane painted bright yellow with an open cockpit. Those were my favorite because they were highly maneuverable and you could feel the wind in your face, hear it whooshing and whistling through the wire struts that held the bi-wings together. There was a romance to it. Just like the "Ol Red Baron," I wore a leather helmet and goggles as I flew all over the area and practiced short takeoffs and landings. Short landings had to be within 50 feet. This was training us to land on beaches and short dirt runways in the Pacific Theater and on aircraft carriers out at sea. We also had to show we could maneuver the plane expertly in the air. We flew up to 3,000 feet to do acrobatics, Immelmann turns (also known as a roll-off-the-top), sack rolls, lines, loops and hammerheads.

Flying a Yellow Peril solo, 1943

We first learned acrobatics with an instructor. It made me nauseous at first. A lot of guys got sick from the rolls and motion. But I kept myself from throwing up, because if I knew if I did, I'd get washed out, and I was determined to complete my training. Even when I started doing the loops and turns by myself, I felt sick. But every day, I went up and rolled, again and again, fighting the urge to vomit until I got over it. It was tough, but after that, I enjoyed doing acrobatics.

There was a lot at stake. Besides throwing up, if you were in an accident, hit a wingtip upon landing or anything like that, or if you flew down in a way that didn't please the instructor, you washed out. If you flunked any of the ground school courses, navigation or radio communication, you washed out. We had to be able to send Morse code at 25 words a minute and receive and translate 25 words a minute. That was very difficult. We learned that in six weeks, but guys that couldn't do it didn't make it. Only about 20% of the class remained after the 18 months of training, only one out of five guys.

I worked hard and never crashed, but one time, I was sure I was going to die.

Hanging Upside Down in Peril

It was a cold day, about twenty degrees out, and I was flying on my own in a yellow Peril wearing a leather jacket with cuffs and gloves trying to stay warm in the open cockpit. My task was to practice my aerobatics starting with a snap roll then a slow roll, recovering at the top of the loop to go up into another loop and turn it over again.

I did the snap roll and the slow roll. Those are fun, and I had gotten good at them. I came up to recover on the top of the loop, upside down. Suddenly, the cuff of my jacket caught the safety belt release knob, and down I fell.

As I started to fall, I caught my elbows on the sides of the cockpit and hung by my toes on the rudder braces, halfway out of the plane. I was upside down flying at 3,000 feet, all by myself, unable to reach the radio or the controls, held up only by my elbows and toes. Inertia kept the little Yellow Peril on a straight plane for the time being, but I had to think quick. I had a parachute on but if I let go, I would lose the airplane and get washed out of aviator training. Besides, the plane could fall anywhere. I looked up into the cockpit above me. The stick, which came out of the floor, was way out of reach. I had to get to that throttle.

I think God was working on my behalf. He must have given me super human strength in my legs and arms at that moment. Fighting gravity, I edged my way further up into the cockpit, a little further, a little further until I could finally reach the stick and roll the plane over. As soon as I did, I flopped into my seat, buckled up, took a moment to catch my breath, and flew back to base.

I couldn't tell anybody about what happened (except Fern in a letter). It might threaten the chance of getting my wings. But I kept reliving the incident in daydreams and nightmares alike. It was like when someone is in a car accident. You think to yourself afterwards, "That didn't really happen, did it?" But it definitely did!

With my squadron. First row, left, 1944

Physical Rigor at the University of Georgia

Next, I went to Pre-Flight School on the University of Georgia campus in Athens, where we had both ground and air training.

Under-attended and financially-troubled, the college was pleased to get the Navy contract for use of their facilities, one of five such schools taken over by the Navy between 1942 and 1945 for this next round of training. Approximately 20,000 cadets trained at these colleges in the skills needed as combat pilots and their crew in the Pacific theater of World War II. The Navy utilized most of the existing campus and built numerous buildings and athletic facilities used by the college in later years. Additional Athens-area sites were also utilized and improvements were made to local streets and Ben Epps Airport. When the war ended, it all went back to civilian hands, and so there are few physical reminders of the large Naval presence that was once there.

On the ground, we learned survival techniques, walking with 50-pound packs through the woods and building fires. It was in the classroom at University of Georgia where I learned Morse code as well.

The physical training program was rigorous. They wanted us to swim five miles in a swimming pool with our clothes on. I still wasn't a strong swimmer, but of course I didn't say, "I can't do that."

Along with the other guys, I jumped in the pool with my clothes on and started moving. As I swam close to one side of the pool, they'd poke me away with a pole, then I'd swim back the other way where they did the same thing on the other edge so you couldn't linger. It was exhausting, but I was young. You have all this energy when you're young. I made it. I also had to jump 20 feet off a tower with all my clothes on and swim. After that, I decided, of course, I could swim! (This opened up a lot of water sports to me later that I love, including waterskiing and diving.)

During flight training, I continued to box. In Georgia, with physical fitness being a priority, I trained in the ring often, pounding on a punching bag and jumping rope. I was a welter weight. The top limit is 148 pounds, and I tried to get to the top

Boxing (right), that time just for fun on a Florida beach, 1945

of my weight. I always kept in very keen shape. But even so, I've never been so tired in my life compared to after a boxing match. After a few rounds, my gloves would get so heavy, I couldn't hold them up. But the same was true for the other guy.

I boxed several times in the armory at the various bases where I was stationed with 100 or 200 guys watching, needing any form of entertainment. For me, that took a lot of courage, because it was in front of an audience. The men would pay five or ten cents to get in. If I was scheduled to box Sunday afternoon, I'd worry about it the entire day before and didn't sleep well. I generally won as many as I lost.

In the Clouds Above Georgia

In Georgia, we learned to fly in formation and tried out heavier planes, and I became a squadron leader. We flew AT6's or the North American Aviation T-6 Texan, an American single-engine, 600-horse power advanced trainer aircraft.

Flying High

The Army and the Navy both used it, but the Navy called them SNJ's. (S = Scout, N = Navy, J= North American with the 1 representing the first trainer built for the Navy by North American.) After World War II, by the way, both branches of aviation were combined into the Air Force.

We called the SNJ a "greenhouse with sliding windows!" It was all metal, a monoplane with retracting landing gear, very maneuverable. We learned to dog fight and bomb targets in those.

Flying with my squadron in T-6's, 1944

Sixty-nine flight hours were expected during basic training in training planes such as the N3N and the T-6 Texan. Then another 28 in intermediate training, 18 hours after were assigned to a specific type of plane, like a bomber or a fighter. Obsolete combat aircraft were used for those, providing an experience close to the real thing while not using up planes that were needed in battle. At the advanced level, flight training included formation flying and gunnery.

Squadron Leader, Brushy Bill

As we started flying in formation, I was assigned to be a squadron leader, in charge of forty-five or so pilots and their crews. Some of the guys in my squadron seemed to look up to me, because I had a couple of years of college and was known to be a good pilot. I worked hard at it. I also worked hard to build their trust.

A ground crew of four men was assigned to each plane. They were in charge of rolling out the planes and checking the tires and the engines and the general condition of each plane. When the pilots arrived, the crewmen saluted, and the airplanes sat in rows on the tarmac, humming up, ready for us to jump in and fly them. The funny thing was I often had a toothbrush sticking out of my mouth when I greeted my crew!

I like to brush my teeth. I'm nuts about it really. My mother taught me to get up from the table and brush my teeth after every meal. I maintained that habit my entire life, receiving great benefits, namely a good smile and good dental health. But I also had the habit of leaving the toothbrush in my mouth afterwards, chewing on it a bit.

Well, the first time it happened, the crew looked at me funny but were afraid to say anything, except one of the guys, who was a little friendlier with me.

Brushy Bill

"Sir, you'd better take that toothbrush out of your mouth," he said. I can still hear it. Of course, I always pocketed the toothbrush before I got in the cockpit, but my habit earned me the nickname "Brushy Bill."

Finding a Spot in the Ocean

I had great fun flying. I enjoyed every minute of it, even the tests. One day, my commanding officer said, "Okay, Bill. Take these four planes and fly out over the ocean. This is where you're going to go." He just wrote down the coordinates, latitude and longitude. That was it. He didn't tell me what was out there. That was the mission, just to find the spot. Off we went, the four other pilots flying behind me in formation.

Though each plane could take two people, we flew solo. We liked it that way. But it meant we had to be our own navigator. We had pencils, paper, and little desktops in our pilot position, which we used to calculate times and directions and winds and determine how far out we were. The desk had a screen on which we could tell somewhat where we were in relation to where the carrier or land was, the plane represented by a dot on the screen. I did the math along the way with the others following, relying on me.

We flew for about an hour and twenty-five minutes with nothing around us but sky, nothing below us but cold, ocean water. Then I spotted the target. A plane had crashed out and was partially submerged. That was the X that marked the spot, and we found it with no outside assistance. That was the test. We circled around the downed plane, and I radioed my squadron to follow me back to base where we arrive safely. I'm still proud of that.

Landing on Aircraft Carriers on Lake Michigan

Next it was back to Illinois, this time to Chicago to Glenview Naval Air Station where I flew Dauntlesses, Wildcats, Hellcats, and Corsairs. We did a lot of flying there and learned even trickier maneuvers, including many spot landings on the runway.

In light aircraft, we had to land in a small circle only about 20 feet across. In order to achieve this, I learned to bring the plane down slowly and straighten it out just in time to bring it down and stop in the circle. We called these hops. They were very difficult but fun. A lot of fun! In winter it snowed, leaving about three feet of snow on the ground. They shoveled it off, and we landed on ice on the runway.

In formation with my squadron

USS Sable (IX-81) underway on Lake Michigan (USA) in 1944

Just like in the Yellow Perils, it was a little uncomfortable up there in our open cockpits in freezing temperatures, but you do what you have to do.

After a series of successful hops, we put our skills to the test taking off from and landing on an aircraft carrier. It was a complex act of coordination. Glenview had two aircraft carriers on Lake Michigan, the U.S.S. Wolverine and the U.S.S. Sable. I was excited when it was my first time to land on one of the carriers. I knew I could do it. When you're nineteen, you know you can do anything.

Each simulated carrier was about as long as a football field, about 400 feet. Landings took place near the stern, take offs near the bow. I can still see that carrier as I came in for a landing, an LSO, Landing Signal Officer directing me with paddles and hand gestures. Just like in the hops, I'd come in real slow, just above stall speed, angled like a duck with the back end of the plane dragging so, as I landed, I could catch a cable called the arresting gear with a steel tail hook fitted to the rear of the aircraft. We had a six-foot radius in which to land. If successful I'd cut the engine and stall the plane at the last minute, and come to a sudden halt. The timing was precarious. You didn't want to fall out of the sky by stalling too early, and you had to catch that cable.

If you didn't catch the wire, then the landing officer would give you the wave off, and you had to give the plane increasing throttle to go back up into the air and try again. You'd better take off correctly to get airborne. The other alternative was to go off the end of the carrier into the water, which could lose you a plane, your Navy wings, or even your life. Aircraft landings were definitely the hardest thing to do in training.

After landing, we either put the plane away down below or received instructions to join another group of flyers, sometimes in a different aircraft. Take offs were fun too. Hydraulic catapults in a track on the surface of the carrier shot us forward from a standstill to take-off speed quickly.

My fellow flyers crashed a few planes. They took off and stalled or did something wrong and came down on the deck. A few times, they flew right into the ocean. I had at least two friends who died in the attempt.

> ### *The Unique Fresh Water Aircraft Carriers*
>
> The U.S.S. Wolverine was originally the Seeandbee launched in 1912 as a Great Lakes luxury side-wheel steamer cruise ship for the Cleveland and Buffalo Transit Company. The U.S.S. Sable was originally built as the passenger ship Greater Buffalo, also a sidewheel excursion steamer. Both ships were purchased by the Navy in 1942 and converted to training aircraft carriers to be used on the Great Lakes. Lacking a hangar deck, elevators, and armament, they were not true warships, but provided advanced training of naval aviators in carrier takeoffs and landings. The Sable and Wolverine hold the distinction of being the only freshwater, coal-fired, side paddle-wheel aircraft carriers used by the United States Navy.

One of them, new at carrier landings and take-offs, had landed and was waved off again. He was only about 50 feet off the deck and hit the throttle, opening it up to full. Unless you roll your cab back to compensate for the torque, your plane's going to twist over with that sudden force. He didn't roll back, and it was too much power coming out of that low speed, and his plane just flipped over, and he was killed.

That evening I was out drinking with the guys. I learned to drink beer during those training years, though I never did like it much. One of the guys said, "Well, you know, in the squadron over there, Pete Jones, he didn't make it today."

We had been out laughing and joking around with Pete the night before, and he was dead the next day. That's how quick it happened. That was hard, losing friends to accidents. The only thing that made it a little less sad was thinking of all of the soldiers and sailors already in combat, many of whom had or would lose their lives fighting for our country and for liberty. A perspective like that brings a little seriousness into your life.

A Wildcat that I flew in training, 1944

A Letter from Lorry

Still, there was some treasured contact between soldiers and their families via letters. I wrote all the time to my parents and my girlfriend Fern, who I would soon marry. Fern also got letters from her brother Laurence, who they called Lorry. He was serving in the infantry on the battlefields in Germany and France, where many men were lost. Here is part of one letter:

December 1944
Dear Fern,
Seems like I just wrote to you but I know my last letter was to Dorothy. Confidentially, I did suffer one screwy thing because of my combat, which I have not shaken off yet. My memory is very poor. Can't remember names one tenth as good as I used to. I believe after some more rest and quiet I'll return to ordinary. In my letter to Betty today I brought up a new subject which hadn't occurred to me until that phase of combat I went through. What would I do if I returned to civilian life before the war is completed? That's a comforting but confusing thought. I can't settle my mind on that question now, but I may consider it before many weeks. I can't see why this war should last much longer. Won't that be a wonderful day when Germany says, "I want to settle things, without further fighting." I have prayed for the end, within a few days, when I was up there, but all of a sudden, I found myself in Holland. I really wanted the war to end for everyone. Whether or not it will end for me depends if I am sent up to the frontline foxholes again. Since I've prayed, I was sent back to the rear and was placed on non-combat duty. I believe God completely answered my prayer, and I'll never see those days of hell again...

Flying High

WWII Dive Bombers

The Douglas SBD Dauntless was the United States Navy's main carrier-based scout/dive bomber from mid-1940 through mid-1944. The SBD was also flown by the United States Marine Corps, both from land air bases and aircraft carriers. The SBD is best remembered as the bomber that delivered the fatal blows to the Japanese carriers at the Battle of Midway in June 1942. The plane earned its nickname "Slow But Deadly" (from its SBD initials) during this period.

The Helldiver, a carrier-bomber, was manufactured for the Navy to replace the Dauntless, but generally neither pilots nor aircraft carrier captains seemed to like it. By reputation it had difficult handling characteristics. Crew nicknames for the aircraft included the Big-Tailed Beast or just the derogatory Beast, Two-Cee, and Son-of-a-Bitch 2nd Class.

Dive Bombing in a Dauntless

Around that time, I started training in dive-bombing, most frequently in a Dauntless aircraft, along with the newer Curtiss SB2C Helldiver, a faster but less maneuverable plane than the Dauntless, and that became my specialty.

Now, that was thrilling, dive-bombing! We would take off from the carrier with our squadron of bombers and fighters. Sometimes a squadron would be forty-five planes in nine or ten flights consisting of four or five planes per flight. We were given orders to fly to some point on the map, some target. For the sake of practice, it might just be a rock or log floating in the water that represented the ship we were ordered to sink. We carried live, small bombs about a foot and a half long, like a small rocket. It was fun. I was nineteen, up in the air at 15,000 feet leading a team of guys, with some flying experience under my belt, confident, and all of a sudden over that target, I would point the nose of my plane straight down towards the earth and release a bomb, which came out of the front of the plane. As squadron leader, the other fellows followed my lead when I said, "Drop!" on the radio.

You had to know when to release that bomb. Inertia will keep it moving forward in trajectory and not directly below you. You had to consider the wind and the speed of both the plane and the target. Judging the distance was one of the things we learned in the classroom. I felt pretty good about it.

When the bombs hit, they exploded, and you could see where you hit, then you pulled up and flew back to the aircraft or back to base. Without lives at stake, it was like a real-life video game.

But the intensity of the training was very real. I wrote to Fern, "I think I've changed more in the last five months than I have in the five years before that."

Chicago, 1944

Fighter Training

I also trained to fight in Wildcats and Hellcats, and a Corsair too, but not as often. For fighter training, one of the pilots in our squadron had to volunteer to tow our target, a large, marked cloth about four feet by twenty feet on a rope billowing out behind his plane. Nobody liked to tow the target, because it was boring, so we took turns. The rest of us would approach him at a perpendicular and use our machine guns to hit the target. We had 50 caliber machine guns in the wings and 20-millimeter cannons. We also got to shoot rockets, which were new at the time in 1943. That was the boyhood dream, flying these planes. It was probably the most thrilling exercise of my life.

Enjoying Chicago

I had good camaraderie with the other guys. In the evenings when we were off-duty, we'd ride the "L" into town to our favorite tavern and often take the last L back home. We didn't have to get back to the dormitories until midnight. Though I continued to drink a little beer with the others, I didn't grow to like it any better. I don't even like it now. Most of the guys liked it a lot. I loved Chicago though, absolutely loved it. The people were so nice. Generally, people showed great respect to us in our uniforms as aviators and officers-in-training, and there were lots of things to do. On base, they showed a lot of movies.

Folks Back Home

All the while that I was in training and Bob was serving as an Army officer in Georgia, my parents were back home in Albany sharing in the hardship of war as all civilians did. They had rationing of all sorts. Meat was rationed, affecting the family business. Milk and a lot of other groceries were rationed. Gasoline was rationed.

Civilians had curfews. Everyone had to be home at certain hours and were required to have black out curtains at night in case of an air raid. Albany took this very seriously and according to a state report "was black and infractions of the rules were rare." They had air watches, civilian patrols looking for airplanes approaching in order to warn people in time to take cover. After Pearl Harbor, an attack by air or submarine by the Japanese on the west coast was plausible.

There was mystery and tension as civilians lacked information about how battles were going. The news was censored. Today when there is war, TV cameras are there right on the spot, live. But there wasn't television then. We depended on letters for communication, and the military took the stance that those could be intercepted by the enemy.

With a proud but worried mother during a brief leave in Albany, 1944

With Fern and my dad

Intelligence officers would read soldiers' letters before they were sent home and black out or cut out parts they didn't want anybody to read, any information they thought might help the Germans or Japanese, names of places where the soldiers were writing from, anything about upcoming plans. It was all pretty tightened down. This was especially stressful when it was your son, brother, husband or father fighting overseas.

Every able-bodied male was in the service. It was compulsory if you were between the age of 18 and 35. Depending upon your physical condition and health, you were classified as a 1A, 2A, 3A, etc. If you were physically incapable of serving somehow, you were categorized 4F. All the rest served in civilian service if not in the military or for the government in some function. People in essential industries like some doctors, some farmers, and some manufacturers were exempted from military service but their work still supported the war effort.

A United Country

It was a tough time with the rationing, restrictions, worries about loved ones and about the country in general and the fate of the world, not nearly like England, which was bombarded, but still hard. It drew everyone in this country more closely together, and some good came from it. It nourished more patriotism and the unity of the entire population. I can't think of a time in history during my lifetime when the people of the U.S. united together more strongly. That includes the Vietnam War, Korean War, the Persian Gulf and all the other conflicts and times of peace since then. I never knew a patriotism like that could exist, that the entire country would try so hard to reach an objective all together. We've lost that now. In the last few decades, I have seen people moving in different directions and factions. I'm not saying we need another war to keep us together, not at all, but we need some national motive to keep us together, to strive together as a nation, as one people.

Letters to Fern

Fern and I were going steady all while I was in training, and I was very much in love with her, so I wrote her many, many letters. Having learned to write for my high school paper and for the community paper, I knew how to express my love for her. Or at least I tried! She kept the letters. Reading them now brings it all back, new love, the pain of being apart, the elation of a reunion, the joy of reading her declarations of love for me. While I was away, another young man tried to steal her away, but Fern chose me.

On leave and engaged! 1944

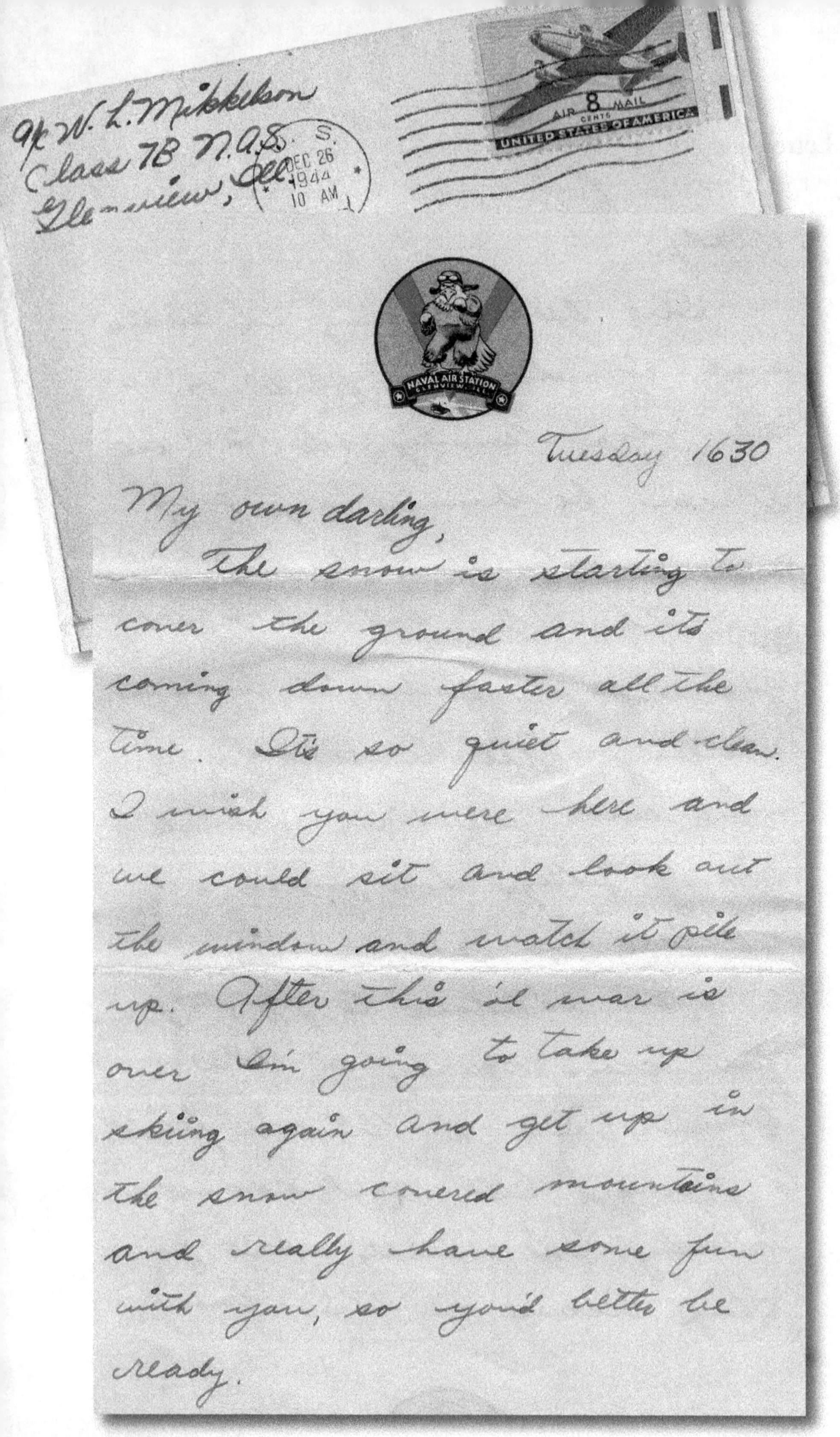

A/c W. L. Mikkelson
Class 7B N.A.S.
Glenview, Ill.
U. S.
DEC 26
1944
10 AM
AIR 8 CENTS MAIL
UNITED STATES OF AMERICA
NAVAL AIR STATION
GLENVIEW, ILL.

Tuesday 1630

My own darling,

The snow is starting to cover the ground and its coming down faster all the time. Its so quiet and clean. I wish you were here and we could sit and look out the window and watch it pile up. After this 'ol war is over I'm going to take up skiing again and get up in the snow covered mountains and really have some fun with you, so you'd better be ready.

A/C W.T. Mikkelson
18-45 cc NAAS
Beeville, Texas

NAVAL AUXILIARY AIR STATION
CHASE FIELD
BEEVILLE, TEXAS

Tuesday 1930

My darling,

I did get a letter from you today so now I'm happy again. Just like a kid with a new toy, but I'd rather play with you than the toy. Is that o.k., honey? I'm sure gettin' lonesome for you, baby and the next ten days are going to creep by.

There's an empty sack above me in our room. How about moving in? I'd have to give you a lift so you could get up there and you'd probably roll off during the night because they're real narrow. I don't think I'd get much sleep.

The End of Training and the End of War, Corpus Christie, Texas

In my dress whites

My next base was the Naval Air Station Corpus Christi in Texas. By then, I was known as a competent dive bomber and was well used to being a military man.

With my training in the air completed, I checked out of my squadron. All we had left was ground school: two gunnery classes, a test, and 100 rounds of shooting. By then, there were only four of us left from the original 21 cadets.

As cadets, we wore simulated officers' uniforms, one of four, depending upon the activity: Khakis, grays, whites and our dress blues. The dress uniform was worn over a white shirt and black tie and included a hat similar to that of a policeman with a white top and a gold braid around the front. We felt pretty snazzy in those, although we looked forward with great anticipation to graduation day, when we would get our official uniforms and our gold wings.

A Few Demerits

No matter what you were wearing as a cadet, your shoes had better be shined. If they weren't or if your room wasn't clean, if there was just a little bit of dust on the dresser or dirt on the floor or your bed wasn't made in regulation-style, you received a demerit. It wasn't unusual to come back to the barracks after flying and find a chit on your bed advising that three demerits had been awarded for one of these offenses. If you were late to a class or an assignment or came in past curfew or didn't stop for a stop sign while driving on base or if you damaged the plane at all while flying, you earned demerits. There were some fellows who washed out because they had too many demerits. I had 50 by the end of training, the most you could get. I was competent but didn't behave very well I guess! One time early in my training, I was late to a class and received a demerit and had to march an additional 50 hours.

The photo of Fern I carried with me throughout training

    I never crashed a plane, but I lost an engine twice. One time in Chicago doing a dive fly, I came up out of the dive, but as I recovered, I blew a cylinder out in the engine. The plane had 12 cylinders, each many cubic inches around and if one goes, the engine stops. Oil spewed out from the hole in the cylinder and blew all over the airplane, the cockpit, the windshield, and my face. I was in the clouds in a stalled airplane weighing 16,000 pounds, trying to join up with my squadron and get back to base. I made it, landing without any engine. It was scary for a while though.

V-Day

On May 8, 1945, known then as V-E Day, Nazi Germany officially surrendered, ending the war in Europe. However, there was still fighting in the Pacific Theatre with the Japanese. The Allies called for unconditional Japanese surrender in the Potsdam Declaration of July 27, but the Japanese government rejected the call. In early August, the USAAF dropped atomic bombs on Hiroshima and Nagasaki, and the Russians invaded and took Manchuria. V-J Day (Victory with Japan) came on August 15, 1945, when Japanese leaders signed an official surrender.

I was very relieved that the war was over, that we were at peace, as was everyone in the country. But I have to admit I was disappointed too. I wasn't going to get to do the job I was trained for. That sounds a little selfish, but I was nineteen years old and had been training hard and was motivated for battled for eighteen months. I was taught to seek out, identify, and bomb enemy aircraft and battleships. I was taught to dislike the enemy and the acts they carried out. We all were. We were trained to be warriors. It was like training for a big game and having the game called off. I wrote to Fern about my true feelings, making her promise not to tell anyone. I knew she would understand.

A photo she sent me in one of her letters

Getting Ready for a Wedding in Texas

With all the letters back and forth and my training complete, I finally said to Fern, "Let's get married," and she enthusiastically replied, "Yes!"

While I was in Beeville in early August 1945, we were already corresponding about what our married life would be like and plans for the wedding. I was so excited. I couldn't wait to put a ring on her finger!

We made plans for her to come out and join me in Corpus Christi, Texas, where I arranged some logistics for our wedding, and she arranged others. Mostly, I had to deal with the administrators in the Navy, and she had to find the church and a reception hall, get flowers and that sort of thing. I got my blood test and our license and met with the chaplain to discuss marriage, including healthy sexual relations. My mother bought our rings and sent them to me in Texas. I was a little disappointed with the rings but knew we could always replace them. Announcements were printed in both local and Albany papers. Fern came out in mid-August, staying with her sister and brother-in-law Jake Prince.

> ### *Getting Wings at Corpus Christi*
>
> By the end of World War II, more than 35,000 naval aviators had earned their wings at Corpus Christi. The Texas base provided intermediate flight training in World War II, training naval pilots to fly SNJ (North American Aviation T-6 Texan), SNV (Vultee BT-13 Valiant), SNB (Beechcraft Model 18 or Beech Twin), OS2U (Vought OS2U Kingfisher), PBY (Consolidated PBY Catalina), and N3N (the Yellow Peril) type airplanes. In 1944 it was the largest naval aviation training facility in the world, covering 20,000 acres and including 997 hangars, shops, barracks, warehouses and other buildings.

January 15, 1945

A/C W. L. Mikkelson 1 B-45 c(c)
Cadet Reg't N. A. T. B.
Corpus Christi, Texas

My dear Cadet: (and the very dearest of all dears)

    I am enclosing the fingerprints of a young women that claims to know you. She is just a young little thing that doesn't know what is going on. Her name is Fern Morse and she gave you as a reference. Would you please write me a letter and tell me just what you think of her??

    According to the notations on the card, heaven only knows what this world is coming to. (My teacher says that you should never end a sentence with a preposition).

    This office would appreciate it very much if you would give your undivided attention to this matter as soon as it is possible. Miss Morse is in dire need of your comfort and thoughfulness and your complete kindness and also your glowing love. I don't know if you love this girl but she is terribly in love with you. Please don't break her heart because it will take years to mend it and by then she will have lost her youthful beauty and the fact that she is blossomming into a lovely young lady that needs only you to be happy, needs your love.

    I might also point out that she is being very true to you. Her loyalness excedes that of all others. She remains faithfully yours and will always until you tell her you no longer want her. (Which I hope you never, never do) I mean not want her and not that I hope you never want her.

    Quoting from Miss Morse, I'll say "I love you." And she really means it.

                                        Very truly yours,

                                        S. A. Jackson by FAM.
                                        S. A. Jackson, Secretary--Fern Morse
                                        Benton County AAA Committee

Enclosure - 1
SAJ:fm

Mr. and Mrs. Clayton H. Morse
announce the marriage of their daughter
Fern
to
William L. Mikkelson
Ensign, United States Navy
on Wednesday, August the twenty-second
Nineteen hundred and forty-five
Corpus Christi, Texas

Fern stopped to visit family and friends on the way to Corpus Christi, 1945

NAVAL AUXILIARY AIR STATION
CHASE FIELD
BEEVILLE, TEXAS

Wednesday 2030

My darling Fern,

    I hate to write letters, but I'm missing you so much, darling that I just have to talk to you somehow. — Since I started this about 45 minutes have passed for a detailed discussion of world problems, flying, and women. Also various other paltry subjects intervened in the conversation.

    Whattyaknow I got a letter from you today and, honey I think you're very sweet. You're my one and only love, darling and I'm not going to let you wait on me hand and foot after we're married. Hey, this is going to be fun isn't it? Every day I think of a new angle and try to figure it. Things will be much easier though with you to help.

Ray and I went to see the chaplain today and he talked to us for over an hour about all aspects of marriage. He's from Oregon, so we were well acquainted from the start.

First we talked about legal business. No physical exam is needed for the girl, but I think it's a good idea anyway. I can get the license alone and have to take a blood test. That's all there is to it.

Then he started on religion for just a few minutes and spent the rest of the time on sexual relations and how to make them happier.

NAVAL AUXILIARY AIR STATION
CHASE FIELD
BEEVILLE, TEXAS

I wish you had been there, darling. He usually talks to both people at once and never leaves out one thing. It was really a good talk and Ray and I were deeply impressed.

He even recommended two books on sex life and we sent for them. I've read two little books in the last week about it. You're probably getting educated firsthand from Dot and Jake. When we get together we should do well don't you think?

I'm getting anxious to have the rings arrive. Shall I send you one or wait. I'd rather put it on you myself. Darn, I wish I'd had it about a year ago and I would have them.

This morning Jack and I flew to San Antonio and got back 20 minutes late so have a 1000 word theme to write on being late getting in. We were late out and that's why, but had a big time looking over all the air fields and places at S.A.

Honey, we just hafta have a waffle iron. Gosh, what will we eat for Sunday breakfast? Maybe we can be lucky enough to find one someplace.

I hadn't thought of what we'll do with an extra few days if I do get them. What ideas do you have? Let's hit the sack, baby!!

I love you much.
                      Your Bill

Shiny Wings and a Beautiful Wife

I had my official graduation from Naval Flight Training and married Fern on the same day, August 22, 1945. What a day! In the morning, I received my wings and by the end of the day, I was a married man.

Even with the war over when my class of cadets earned our gold wings, it felt awfully good. We became officers with the rank of ensign, the equivalent to a lieutenant in the Army, receiving our naval aviation greens. Other than Marine officers, we were the only service branch of the military to wear greens. On them we pinned our wings proudly. Stripes on the epaulets signified that we were officers and fully trained pilots. One stripe meant you were an ensign. A stripe and a half signified you were a lieutenant junior grade. Two stripes meant you were a lieutenant, and four stripes a lieutenant captain. Eventually in the reserves, I reached the rank of lieutenant captain before I mustered out.

In my officer greens with my wings

After graduation, we ate in the officer's mess where we were waited on by people wearing white uniforms. Walking along the streets on the base, everyone saluted us. It was easy to get a little cocky.

As a cadet, I made $75 a month. That was a lot of money to me in those days. They fed and housed us, and no taxes were taken out of our pay. I saved most of the money. When I got my wings, my salary went up to $85 a month, which seemed to me like a fortune. Plus, we had a food allowance. This was important since I would soon be supporting a wife.

Travel was still difficult with the war newly ended, so our families didn't come out for the ceremony, which took place in the First Presbyterian Church, a small church, in the evening at 8:15 p.m. Dorothy and Jake Prince were in attendance, along with friends.

Immediately following the ceremony, we had a reception and late dinner in the terrace room of the Robert Driscoll Hotel, a towering and grand 18-floor hotel on the bluff overlooking town (built in 1942). We hired a DJ, and everybody had a good time. The friends at the festivities were mostly stationed in Corpus Christie. Guests included a few friends from home who were stationed in the area and a couple new friends I made in training. It was a wonderful day!

Robert Driscoll Hotel
Corpus Christi · Texas

A wedding of interest in Albany and Corvallis is that of Miss Fern Morse, daughter of Mr. and Mrs. C. H. Morse of Corvallis, and Ensign William Mikkelson, son of Mr. and Mrs. Harry Mikkelson of Albany, on Wednesday, August 22, at 8:15 o'clock in the evening, at Corpus Christi, Texas, at the First Presbyterian church. The Rev. Tucker read the service.

The bride, presented in marriage by her brother-in-law, Lt. Jake Prince of Albany, wore a white silk jersey dress with sweetheart neckline and a short white veil. She carried a white Bible with a white orchid and carnations and on the streamers were bits of fern.

Mrs. Jake Prince, sister of the bride, was her honor attendant, and she wore a chartreuse shaded silk dress with black accessories and a corsage of white carnations.

Ensign Luke Morin acted as best man.

Immediately following the ceremony a reception and dinner was held in the Terrace room of the Robert Driscoll hotel.

Guests at the wedding were 1st Lt. and Mrs. Cully Carlson, Portland, Or.; Miss Patricia Stuart, specialty T3/c of the WAVE, Albany, Ore.; Lt. and Mrs. Jack L. Bird, Albany, Ensign Leo E. Brown, naval air corps, New York; Ensign John Cook, New York, and Ensign Joe Drabb of Long Island, N.Y.

Ensign Mikkelson, a graduate of Albany high school, was graduated from the naval air corps school the morning of the wedding. He will be stationed in Florida. He is a former student at Oregon State college and is a member of Sigma Nu fraternity.

Mrs. Mikkelson was graduated from Corvallis high school and attended Oregon State college and is a member of Kappa Kappa Gamma sorority.

Ensign and Mrs. Mikkelson left for Georgia to visit Ensign Mikkelson's brother and wife, Lt. and Mrs. Robert Mikkelson, before Ens. Mikkelson leaves for Florida.

August 22, 1945. A very happy day

Enjoying our wedding reception with Fern's sister (head of table) and friends

Another element of that happy day, my Aviator license

Arrested on My "Honeymoon"

We didn't have what you would call a honeymoon, but I was to be stationed for a short time before my discharge in Florida, so we stayed in a motel that night, and left the next morning on a train for Columbus, Georgia, to visit my brother, Lieutenant Robert Mikkelson and his wife Shirley on our way south. Bob was stationed at Fort Benning, the largest infantry training school in the world.

One day while Fern and I were staying with Bob and Shirley, we had Bob's car, a very nice coupe. Not all people owned cars then with the war, but Bob had held on to his to help make things easier with a wife and young family. We were looking after their baby Judie and had her in a car seat in the backseat on an errand in Columbus, I don't remember what, and were on our way back to their house when all of our newlywed joy was tested in one tense moment.

At Bob and Shirley's house in Georgia

Late August, 1945

To this day there is a love-hate relationship between the townies and servicemen there in Columbus, which is located on a stretch of the muddy Chattahoochee River that separates Georgia from Alabama. For the most part, they just hated servicemen at the end of World War II. Even though the young men training at Fort Benning were fighting for our country, the locals saw them as outsiders that often misbehaved in town during their off-hours. It was also a large base, so there were a lot of enlisted men coming and going all the time.

Well, I stopped at a crosswalk to let a pedestrian cross, and once she had gone past the car, I started forward. Immediately, a siren wailed and two officers in a police car pulled me over. Evidently, the pedestrian had one foot on the curb and had the other foot still on the street when I moved forward. She was, of course, well out of the way of the car and safe, but that didn't matter to them. Those policemen had me step out the car. Naturally, I was wearing my leather jacket with my wings on it. They arrested me, taking me away from Fern and our baby niece in the back, took me to jail, put me in a cell and slammed the door. I can still hear the slamming of that metal door. And then they left me there alone. Nobody tended to me. Nobody talked to me. It was in the middle of the day. Fern must've called my brother or hurried back to his house with Judie to get his help, but I knew nothing of this, stranded in that cell, not knowing how long they were going to hold me there.

I was in jail for what felt like forever but was probably about an hour before Fern, driving the coupe, Judie safely left with Shirley at their home, came to pick me up. The police fined me $15, which was quite a bit of money on a serviceman's pay.

Though it was a disturbing event, it was over quickly. Fern and I were reunited, and though I was mad about it, that faded too, leaving just a story to tell, one of the first challenges of our married life together.

A Black Eye in Florida

After our stay in Georgia with Bob, Shirley and Judie, Fern stayed to visit friends, while I reluctantly left her and took the train to the Naval Air Station in Pensacola, Florida, to check in to my "final" assignment. It helped that I was there with the boys, all of us new pilots, four of my buddies from prior training. In Pensacola, we did more flight training, which had a different tenor to it with the war over. During that time, we had to decide whether to continue a career in the military or return to civilian life. I looked forward to talking it over with Fern.

But first things first. One of my tasks during off hours that first week was to find a place to live with my new wife, which I did. I was ready to greet her to our first "home" together when she got to Pensacola.

She was to arrive on the train the next Saturday evening. That Saturday afternoon, the boys and I had time off and were looking for something to do. I had to keep busy. I was so excited with the anticipation of Fern's arrival I had to do something to occupy my mind and while away the time. I suggested we rent some horses and go riding on the beach. I don't exactly remember where I got the idea, maybe we just passed a stable while walking around.

We rented four horses. While choosing our steeds, the lady who trained the horses said, "Who gets the wild one?"

The other three guys voted that I should have it, because I was from the "Wild West." They were all from New York or other Eastern cities. To them, Oregon was the Wild West!

The riding was great fun. After trotting along for a while, getting accustomed to our horses, we decided to have a race. My horse was the fastest and I was the most experienced rider, so I raced ahead, galloping at full, 20 miles per hour though it seemed like a hundred. A couple hundred yards from our appointed finish line, I leaned out to the side of the horse's head to see what was coming up, passed over a ditch and suddenly my saddle gave way.

The girth, the belt around the horse's torso, had never been buckled. Down I went, saddle and all, hitting my head on the berm of the trail and rolling over into the grass.

My horse kept going. The other guys couldn't stop theirs either, but as soon as they could, they came back and picked me up. I was okay, nothing broken, but as time passed, the bruises started to show. I had a horrible black eye and purple skin all down my cheek. I looked just terrible, a little bloodied and scarred too. And wouldn't you know it, it was time for the guys to take me to the train station to meet my bride.

With a black eye, about to meet my new bride at the train station, 1945

When I saw her, I went to give her a kiss. She looked at me aghast.

"What have you been doing?" she asked, "Have you been in a fight?"

"I fell off a horse," I told her.

"No, you didn't," she said at first, not knowing whether I was lying to her or not, until I told her all the details and the other fellows corroborated my story.

Newlyweds in Florida

Fern and I stayed in Pensacola about three months in the rented furnished apartment that I found for us before she arrived. Each day when I woke up, it was beside my beautiful wife, making it a truly memorable time while I finished my training. It didn't hurt having the beach and warm ocean water and sunshine. On weekday mornings, we'd awake to the revving engines of the dive-bombers that I would be flying that day. Even though they were a mile away, they were as loud as could be. They were great big engines, sixteen-cylinders and powerful. Fun to fly. I'd get into my uniform, kiss my wife good-bye, and go drop some bombs.

Even though our troops were pulling out of war-torn regions, we still had to be ready for anything. The American Armed Forces were setting up new bases in what had been enemy territory. I was a dive-bomber and skilled pilot that the Navy invested into, and

they weren't ready to let go of me just yet. If you're going to hit targets dive-bombing, it takes continual practice. So, in Pensacola, we trained as if we might still be deployed. Our squadron got even better at judging perspectives and perfecting the time to release the bombs. It was difficult and inexact at that time, so even in advanced training, we didn't actually hit the targets very often, but when we did, it was quite a rush.

We had a wonderful time as newlyweds during those three autumn months in Florida, 1945

Newlyweds in Florida, 1945

Back to Civilian Life

As newlyweds, it was a very happy time in Pensacola. On weekdays, I flew, deepening my lifelong passion for flying. Weekends were spent playing on the beach with friends or just in each other's company. Fern and I talked about our immediate future and decided to go home where I'd finish my military obligation by serving in the reserves for three years in Oregon.

Three months later, we said good-bye to the Florida sunshine, an admiral shook my hand at my honorable discharge, and Bill and Fern Mikkelson headed back to Albany to settle into our civilian life together.

With our first baby Bobbie, 1947

Chapter Six

Young Married Life
1946 to 1957

ONCE I WAS DISCHARGED FROM THE NAVY, Fern and I returned to Albany to set up house, renting our first home at 433 W. 4th Street. We didn't have a lot of money, but Fern had some saved up and so had I, and it didn't take much to get by with just the two of us. I transitioned into my role as a bread winner, not thinking about it much really. It's just what we did in those days as young men.

My father wanted Bob and me to work with him at Harry's Market, of course. Neither of us wanted to necessarily, but we both needed a steady income. Bob had Shirley and Judith. Fern and I planned on starting a family too. And the shop was a family obligation or inheritance (depending on how you looked at it). The only problem was my father was used to having Bob and I work there for free.

My mother was very helpful in the situation. She said to my dad, "They are married men. You employ them. You've got to pay them, Harry." So, I resumed my work as a meat cutter, hauling and preparing and cutting meat in the shop, now full-time.

With Fern in Albany, 1946

Bob worked the counter. At the same time, we both looked for other opportunities. I knew I didn't want to stay in the butcher shop forever, so I came up with an idea for my own business, the first of many as it turned out.

Mountains to Climb, Fields to Dust

There were many farms in the vicinity around Albany, including my father-in-law's, and I had the idea to start a crop-dusting business. I called it the Aero-Dusting Company. A friend and I went in together, pooled our money and bought a Piper Cub that was out in Chicago. They were fairly inexpensive and easy to obtain with so many retired because of the war's end and updated flight technology. Since I was working full-time, the friend agreed to take the train back to Illinois and fly the Cub home.

In the meantime, I started driving out to farms in the evenings persuading farmers to sign up with us to have their fields dusted. I had plenty of takers for our services. No planes or pilots had been readily available during World War II. I told our clients, "I'll dust your fields for $2.00 an acre." Two dollars an acre was really good for me. Our only cost was gasoline for the plane, which was about sixteen cents per gallon, and the farmers provided the dust, a poison for retarding insects.

It took my partner two days to fly the 85-horsepower Piper from Chicago to Albany. Flying the entire way by himself and in a hurry to get back, he tried to stay in the air as long as he could before landing to get some sleep, and we almost lost him and the plane before he ever got to Albany!

In a Cub's dashboard is a fuel indicator that is basically just a horizontal metal piece that looks a bit like a nail perpendicular to another nail-like piece of metal that prevents the indicator from going clear out of sight, a big-T basically. The indicator is simply a floater so it goes down as the fuel goes down. My partner became overly-fatigued. He had been flying for ten hours, following the railroad tracks below him as a guide.

The New Crop Dusting Industry

The first known use of a "heavier-than-air machine" to disperse products occurred on August 3, 1921. The practice was developed under the joint efforts of the U.S. Agriculture Department and the U.S. Army Signal Corps' research station at McCook Field in Dayton, Ohio, to kill a caterpillar that was overrunning crops in that region. But it wasn't until the invention of insecticides and fungicides in the 1930s that crop dusting came into existence and slowly spread in the Americas and, to a lesser extent, other nations. At that time, the substances were actually dust and not liquid and thus the name "crop dusting" came into being. Without planes available during the war, the practice was mostly defunct, resuming with more frequency (and new types of dust) after WWII.

Half-asleep, he looked at the indicator, and in his stupor thought to himself, "Oh no! A telephone pole!" He turned the plane to avoid nothing and darn near crashed. It's a good illustration of how screwed up you can get if you're flying sleep-deprived.

Luckily, he and the plane made it home in one piece. If it had only stayed that way!

By the time he landed our "new" plane in Albany, I had about 2,000 acres signed up at $2.00 an acre. That's equivalent to about $52,000 in 2018, a lot of money for the effort. And, I would be in a business that allowed me to fly and own a plane.

Taking Fern Up in the Cub

I was so excited to fly my own plane over my hometown. Then I took Fern for a ride. A two-seater, she sat in front while I piloted from the seat behind her. We flew down over a grove of tall cottonwood trees over a pond. I wanted to practice getting as low as I could, a necessity for crop dusting.

Crop dusting requires very low flying. You have to practice, bringing the plane down as low as you can, your wheels just touching the grass. If there's a fence, you have to clear it and then bring the plane down rather rapidly in order to cover all the crops. As soon as you're over the fence, you pull the duster lever to let the dust out. At the end of the crop row, you stop the dust, take the plane up and turn it around to hit the next row. You have to do all of this, and you have to do it well. Too low, and you can topple. Too high, and the dust won't hit its mark.

I flew low enough over the pond that the landing wheels spun in the water like mills, the water spraying up on the sides of the plane. Poor Fern was scared to death. After we landed, she said, "Bill, would you mind not doing that again?" She, of course, flew with me many times over the years, and I knew she trusted me, so I never put my wheels in the water like that again while she was my passenger.

A Crop-Dusting Business Dusted

I installed a bin on the plane that would hold and distribute the dust and then my partner and I were ready to dust some fields.

The first field was about forty acres, the size of a golf course. On a Sunday when I didn't have to be at Harry's Market, we filled up the bin with the farmer's dust, and I took to the air. I flew over one row, released the dust over the crops, looped around and dusted the next row. My partner had a broomstick and moved to the end of each row that I was dusting, holding it up to show my turn-around point. It went very well. $80 made!

I landed and told him, "It's your turn."

We loaded up more dust for the next farm, and he took off. We decided we didn't need the broomstick, so I sat down to wait for him. I sat and sat and waited and waited. Something was wrong. It should have only taken him five minutes to get to the next field, twenty minutes to dust, and five minutes to get back. He'd been gone over an hour.

Finally, I took off walking along the highway towards the field he was supposed to have dusted. When a truck approached me from the direction I was headed, I waved it down.

"Did you see anything unusual on the farm you just passed?" I asked the driver.

"Oh, do you mean that airplane that's crashed down there?"

Imagine. My new plane! And my partner! Was he dead?

I asked the truck driver if he'd please take me back where he'd seen this, and he graciously complied. When I saw the plane out in the field, I thanked the driver, jumped the fence and ran as fast as I could through the grass toward the downed Cub.

The plane lay on its side smashed into pieces with the wings broken and leaning on the ground, its wheels up in the air. I rushed to the upturned cockpit. Nobody was in it. I saw no blood either, which was some relief. But what happened? Where was my friend?

He probably got injured so badly that they carried him away, I thought.

There was a farmhouse just up the hill. I thought maybe the folks in there might know something. I ran as fast as I could toward it through a field of flax as high as my knees.

The farm's owner answered the door and invited me in, listened to my frantic questions, and pointed behind him towards the kitchen. There was my partner, sitting at the table drinking coffee, laughing and joking with the farmer's wife. What a jerk! I could have killed him. But at the same time, I was so happy to see he was okay. I hugged him first, then I bawled him out.

We lost our investment. There were probably fifteen farmers waiting for us to dust their fields, and I had to either give them their money back or find another plane. Well, they didn't want their money back. They wanted their fields dusted.

I checked around and found another airplane. This time I rented it—I had no money to buy another—and I hired a different

My crop dusting business rose and fell in little more than a day, 1946.

friend, a fellow I graduated from high school with named Larry Roth (He went on to be Mayor of Albany a decade or so later). He was a trained Navy pilot like me. Again, I would have done the work myself, but I had to work in butcher shop.

The next day, Larry went off to dust his first field. An hour later, he turned up at the market. On foot. He had crashed. He didn't get hurt at least. He was able to walk out, but the rental plane was destroyed.

"Would you please take me out there and show me?" I asked.

He crashed the plane right on the railroad tracks and didn't remember how he actually got himself out of the cockpit uninjured. A few fellows in the area who saw the incident helped him move the plane off the tracks.

I guess neither of my friends were used to the low flying necessary for crop dusting.

I wasn't making much money at the butcher shop, forty-five dollars a week or something like that, just enough to sustain Fern and me and to invest in buying airplanes and crashing them. There I was with a damaged rental plane that couldn't fly. It wasn't completely destroyed, but it wasn't going to dust any crops, and I had to pay for the repairs.

I called up the few competing dusters in the surrounding area that were also starting up post-war, and I handed them all my clients. They were overjoyed. Then I phoned the farmers, as many as I could without going to see them, visited the rest, and gave them the names of the other dusters. The dusting got taken care of, but I certainly didn't get my two dollars an acre.

Stamping Out a Vending Machine Business

My next attempt at additional income was postal vending machines. I don't remember how I learned of the opportunity, but I acquired a few, filled them with stamps, and put them in front of lampposts around town. I made a few dollars a week, but that was all.

It really wasn't profitable. It took time and effort to manage all the machines and some investment dollars that were hard to earn back.

A half a dozen other business ideas that I tried in those early family years didn't work either, but I was never discouraged. I just tried a new one.

Raising a Wonderful Family with Fern

Before long, Fern and I had a family. People can go on and on about what makes them happy, material things, travel, lifestyle. Who knows, counting nails may make some person happy! For me, the greatest happiness involves creating and caring for a family and doing things for them. I just loved it from the first moment of marriage and fatherhood. My entire life, my family has brought me joy. And Fern shared this as her greatest happiness too.

During all those busy early days of trying to create a good living, Fern was home taking care of babies. Bobbie was the first, named after my brother and born in 1947 when Fern and I were just 22 years old. We were so excited to meet her and about the change to our lives. Some fellows like to have a son as their firstborn. I happen to love girls, which was good since Fern and I had four of them

New parents at 22 years old with Bobbie, 1947

before Michael. After little Bobbie, bang, bang, bang, along they came! Chris was next, then Gail, and a little later, Jennifer and Mike.

Before our second, Christine, was born in 1949, we bought a house at 1075 W. Queen Avenue across from the new Albany High School. It was small for our growing family, so even though I'm not particularly handy, I decided to build a room over the garage, which became a fun play area for the kids.

With Bobbie and Chris, 1950

But we outgrew that house pretty quickly with the birth of Gail in 1951 and moved to a larger house four doors down at 1021 W. Queen Avenue. It had three bedrooms upstairs, one downstairs with a big den, one bathroom, and a fireplace perfect for hanging up Christmas stockings. This "newer" home had a furnace fueled by sawdust. It took maintenance to change up the sawdust and keep the house heated, but that was just part of owning a home.

Bobbie, Chris and Gail, 1951

Fern and I both took charge of this, refilling the furnace from a big hill of sawdust we kept in the garage. The girls thought it great fun to climb on the indoor sawdust hill. We updated the furnace a few years later.

Jennifer joined us in 1955.

In 1956, Fern was expecting again. One day after the doctor announced to us that it would be a boy, the doctor and I were out skiing, and he decided he should have a little talk with me. "You know, Bill," he said, "I think it's time to call it N-U-F. I think that's enough."

It was funnier still, because my doctor was a very serious guy. I don't think I ever heard him crack a joke. He looked me right in the eye when he said it. I almost giggled. But Fern and I agreed. Five beautiful children were enough.

Mike, Jennifer, Gail, Chris and Bobbie, our beautiful children in pajamas made by Fern, 1957

Our wonderful family in front of our home on Queen Avenue, 1958

A piggyback ride for Bobbie and Chris after work, 1951

Daily Family Routines

On work days during those years, I had a pretty set routine. I would get up in the morning at 6:00 or so, fix my own breakfast and go off to work, usually before anybody else was up. I fixed myself two soft boiled eggs, one piece of toast, and a small bowl of cold cereal, an easy breakfast that just dirtied one pan. I ate that breakfast for probably twenty years.

In the early days, working at Harry's all day and exploring my other ventures at night and with babies waking during the night, I sometimes came home for lunch and power naps, especially during summer when I could play with the kids for a while. I would lie down on the couch and sleep for sometimes only ten minutes and then get up to go back to work. I got pretty good over the years at rejuvenating with those power naps.

During the Smoke-Craft years, I generally took a sandwich to work. I still worked close to home and could have gone home for lunch, but there was too much to do. By then, the kids were all in school or busy with their own summer activities anyway.

In the evening I would show up at least a half hour before dinner, which was usually around 7:00, and dilly dally and play with the kids. We'd have some fun together

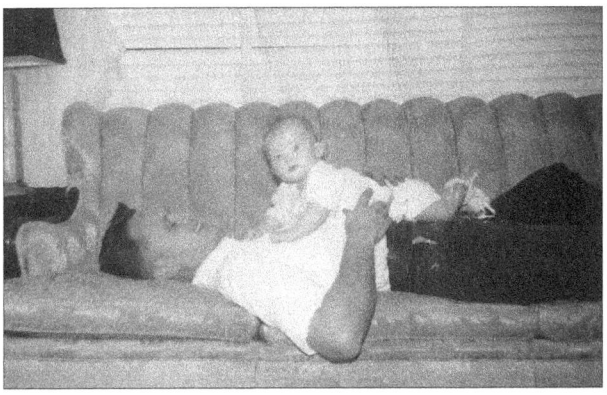

Waking up from a power nap with Gail, 1951

or I'd let them show off new skills or accomplishments or things they had learned, and then we all had dinner together. When we became a family of seven, it was quite a production for Mama! We always said thanks to God and blessed the food before eating.

After dinner, the girls would go in and take a bath before bedtime. I'd supervise them when they were little while they played in the tub. That was fun, watching them splash around, giggling. I enjoyed reading them their bedtime stories too. Being a father is quite rewarding.

Reading to the kids at bed time, Bobbie, Chris and Gail, 1953

My folks with Chris and Bobbie, 1949

The kids had their grandparents around. My mom helped pay for and get the kids to piano music lessons from Mrs. Worley. They all had at least some lessons. I think my mother hoped the next generation might stick with it longer than Bob and I did!

When the kids were old enough, Fern and I gave them a small allowance and started taking them downtown to the bank to make deposits in their own savings accounts, 10 cents, $1.00, whatever they had saved. We wanted them to learn how to work and save.

Fern was marvelously flexible. She sometimes didn't know what meats I would bring home for dinner on any given day. It would depend on what sold that day, what was left, what we had too much of in the market. But we always had the best meats and fresh fish for our meals. We lived so close to the market that she could send the kids to pick up anything we needed, charging it to our account.

Per tradition in both of our families, we had wonderful Christmases. Every year, Fern made a matching set of night gowns for the girls and pajamas for Michael, and we took annual Christmas pictures of the children. It was a nice, steady home life. Fern managed it with expertise.

We had great friends and family around, (left to right) Mervin Stenberg, Dorothy, me, (unknown), Jake, Fern.

Weekend Fun

Saturdays weren't much different from any weekday for me, because I usually worked on Saturdays at Harry's Market and at Smoke-Craft in its early days. Sometimes on Saturday nights, when the kids were old enough, Fern and I'd tuck them in, and we'd go to the Elks Lodge to socialize with friends and dance. I loved that. I became an Elk at a fairly young age.

I saw Bob every day at the shop, and our families got together fairly often (with Bobbie and Judie), 1949

The lodge was a big dance hall with a live orchestra playing swing music. Fern was a good dancer, and I tried my best. We'd usually return home about midnight, with church and Sunday school the next morning.

Sunday, we attended church, and the kids all went to Sunday school. For a while, I taught Sunday school, co-teaching with a lady friend of mine named Nancy. We taught the junior high school-aged girls. It was fairly easy to prepare for class, pretty cursory. We just took turns delving into some of the Bible and telling its stories, and the girls were hungry for or at least receptive to what we had to say. I thoroughly enjoyed teaching Sunday School.

Camping and a Little "Fishy" Trick

At one point, Nancy and I decided we needed an outside activity of some sort for the girls and decided on a camping and fishing trip. The mountains were only some five miles from home. We set up camp beside a stream with five tents housing two or three girls in each tent. The girls were instructed to bring fishing poles with them, but they weren't particularly enthusiastic about fishing. So, I decided to play a little trick on everyone.

In the morning while the girls and Nancy were still asleep, I got up early and pulled from the cooler six trout, which I had bought at the grocery store. I laid out five of them on the bank of the stream. The sixth one I put on a hook and lowered my line into the stream. Then I shouted, "The fish are biting!"

All the girls in the tents heard me. "Oh, my gosh! Oh, oh!" they exclaimed as they hurriedly threw on their shoes, not bothering to change out of their pajamas, grabbed their poles, and came to join me at the creek and throw in their lines. But no one caught a thing, not a bite. When you enjoy fishing and are anticipating catching something, five minutes goes by like that, and thirty minutes can seem like five minutes. But the patience of the girls was pretty short, especially being in their pajamas. They asked me how I caught them, but I never told them about my trick. I always liked playing little pranks.

A Young President of Kiwanis

Along with the Elks, I was in the Albany Kiwanis Club, joining around 1952. My brother and I both still worked at Harry's Market, so when Bob took the classification of Meat Retailer with the local Rotary Club, that meant I couldn't join. So, instead I joined the Kiwanis.

The next year, even though I was just twenty-nine years old, a friend of mine in the club wanted me to run for president. "I'm not going to run for that. I'm too young," I told him, but he nominated me anyway, and I decided to accept the nomination. Lo and behold, I was elected. At the time, I may have been the youngest president our club ever had.

Gov. Paul Patterson told about problems discussed at the recent Governors' conference Thursday when appeared as main speaker at a joint meeting of the Albany Rotary and Kiwanis clubs. He is shown above in conversation with Stan Czech (left), Rotary club president, and Bill Mikkelson, Kiwanis president. (Staff Photo.)

Everybody else was in their 40s or 50s or older.

Ours was a very active service club—we had a great bunch of guys—and of course the work we did was meaningful to me, since I liked to serve our community. As a club, we did a lot! We built a community swimming pool in my presidential year, added a sports center and new dressing rooms. We built an athletic park, started programs for gardening, and did numerous other things.

At the end of my presidential year, our Club was declared the #1 Kiwanis in the Northwest for completing effective service in our community. That was out of some 200 clubs in Washington, Oregon, and Idaho. Winning that recognition was quite a nice surprise for the club and me.

Accomplishing all we did wasn't without challenges at times. Here I was, this young man trying to persuade older gentlemen to attend the luncheon meetings regularly or asking them to lead this city renewal project or serve on that committee. It took a lot of time and management.

Perhaps it helped that I was young. I had energy and enthusiasm. Our church needed help too. The membership was growing, and we needed to double the size of the building, so some of us canvassed our Church membership to finance the addition.

Then there was the campaign for better dental health for our community. That was a big one.

Fluoridation

In the 1940s, we learned what fluoridation could do for our teeth. My kids all received fluoride treatments at the dentist's office. I paid for them. But then we learned we could add fluoride to our drinking water to greatly improve dental health for everyone for free. In 1945, Grand Rapids, Michigan, became the first city to add fluoride to their public water supply. Cavities in children born after the start of fluoridation dropped by more than 60%. I wanted that for our community.

In 1956, Oregon's state supreme court recognized the rights of cities to fluoridate their water. As chairman of the Albany Junior Chamber of Commerce's (Jaycee) civic improvement committee, I convinced the group to co-sponsor a move to get the measure on the May primary election ballot. We had tried in 1952, but it was defeated in the city election. But in 1956, new evidence supported the benefits.

That was one of the biggest campaigns of my life, besides the YMCA (which came a little later). I made over fifteen speeches to the Quantas Club, Kiwanis Club, Rotary Club, the Chamber of Commerce, to schools, a lot of speeches. Just like in high school, I joined the Toastmasters so I would be a better speaker, more persuasive. I was in my twenties, and speaking to groups like the City Council. I had to convince people twenty years, forty years older than me. But I got so I wasn't so terribly bashful. Those speech classes sure helped. I learned when speaking about a subject you learn everything you can about the subject and then you know more about it than your audience. With that expertise, you're teaching them something. That perspective makes it a little easier.

I campaigned to all these civic groups, got fluoridation on the ballot, and this time around, the measure won! Albany got fluoridation in its drinking water.

I was always busy: building businesses and income, helping Fern raise our family, doing community service, volunteering with the church. I even played basketball on the Kiwanis team in the city league, and one year we were city champs. I trained myself to bounce out of bed in the morning, literally. I used to say to myself, "You're going to bounce out of bed." I'd get at the edge of the bed and bounce up. I don't know how I ever got that attitude, but that's what I did.

Of course, I love to be athletic and active. It's good for me, so I always found time to waterski, snow ski, hike, play tennis, and do other sports. During winter in the early years, snow skiing was a favorite.

Kiwanis Club basketball team wins the Albany city championship, 1957
I'm front row, second from left.

Hoodoo Weekends

Throughout my life, I loved snow skiing. As far as recreation is concerned, flying was my first love and snow skiing my second. The nearest skiing to Albany was at Hoodoo Ski Area about eighty miles away on Highway 20. Hoodoo became a frequent weekend destination for the family. Late Saturday afternoon after I finished work, we'd pile into our new Buick station wagon, and hit the road for Hoodoo, skiing all day Sunday, returning home that night. We sometimes met up with friends at Hoodoo and made friends there.

Fern learned to ski with me while we were dating, but she was not in love with skiing. She found it cold, and she wasn't driven to ski the steeper slopes. One time, with her mother babysitting the kids, we went up to Hoodoo, and Fern came back with a broken ankle. That didn't help her love the sport more! She enjoyed the family trips though.

Young Married Life

With Fern at Hoodoo, 1950s

One time when Bobbie was still just a baby, probably about 18 months old, we took her with us to Hoodoo. I went halfway up the mountain, put little Bobbie on my shoulders, and started skiing down.

Suddenly, I stumbled and fell. I knew she was going to fall, so instead of letting her hit the ground or having me fall on top of her, I threw her into the air about ten feet away so she landed in soft, fresh snow. I tumbled and as quick as I could, got up and went to her. She was just fine, but I never did that again!

Shortly after that, I became an instructor at Hoodoo, which made the skiing more affordable for the family, especially during the tight years. In order to get certified, I trained with instructors of the National Ski Association. It took a while to complete the 14 or so days of training to receive my certification since I usually worked six days a week, but I thoroughly enjoyed it. I learned how to do Ski Patrol too. I found ski instruction pretty easy. Most of the time, I'd demonstrate the form for skiing and how to turn—

> **Hoodoo History**
>
> Hoodoo started as a ski area in 1938, funded by a fellow named Ed Thurston, a Eugene-area mill owner who later moved to Bend, Oregon, and was an avid skier. The current 'Big Green Machine' lift follows the same line as the original rope tow. The first chairlift and the three-story Santiam Lodge (with quarters for up to 120 guests) were built using World War II surplus structures around 1946-47 by the CCC (and operated by the United Presbyterian Church in its early years). The cost to stay in the lodge was $1.25 if you brought your own sleeping bag, $3.00 if you didn't. In 1950, Hoodoo introduced the first double chairlift in the state, and one of the first in the world.

starting students off with a "snowplow" with the points of their skis together, then I'd ski down twenty feet and have them ski to me. As they got the hang of it, I'd ski slowly in front of them while they followed.

As soon as the kids were old enough, six years old or so, I put them on the lower slopes and taught them how to ski. As they improved, I took them to the bigger slopes. The skis in those days had wire bindings, the gloves were made of leather, and the girls could get pretty cold sometimes. Still, the kids liked skiing too, and we made great memories together.

One of the perks of being a ski instructor was that my family could stay for free in the old wooden lodge at Hoodoo. We shared a six-bunk bedroom. The hundred-foot long building was pretty rustic with a shared kitchen, but it served the purpose. Once they were built and became available, we rented a cabin that had a kitchen. Hoodoo was a large part of our lives and the kids' childhoods.

The kids (Gail, Chris and Bobbie) and car prepped for a Hoodoo weekend, circa 1955, and (below) in my element! Circa 1950

Duck Hunting

Back from a hunt with Jake, 1957

While skiing and flying and tennis became lifelong pleasures, other activities came and went. For a few years, early every Friday or Saturday morning during the fall hunting season, I went duck hunting with my friend and brother-in-law Jake Prince. It was fun to do that with him and my dog Champ. I only had two dogs during my lifetime, my childhood dog, Tim, who turned out to be a rather big dog, and Champ who was a spaniel. We'd come home with ducks and being the butcher I am, I'd clean them all up, and we'd have a nice duck feed.

I had a few other hunting experiences, like the annual deer bow hunting trip with a bunch of friends and later a little pheasant hunting, but with work demands increasing through the 1960s, I didn't do a lot of that.

My Cub Piper

Despite the crashed planes when trying to start the crop-dusting business, I did acquire my own airplane before too long. Two friends of mine from school days, who both became policemen in town, went in with me to buy one. We each put in $200. It wasn't much of an airplane, another little Cub Piper, but that was the model that was available and affordable. The three of us owned the plane for a while and took turns flying it. After a while though, I was pretty much the only one using it.

One Saturday morning I came home from the butcher shop, and there was a police car out in front. I thought, "What's going on?" When I went in, there were my two partners waiting for me at the kitchen table. One of them said, "Have you got a silver dollar, Bill?"

I said, "No, but I could probably get one."

When I came back with the coin, they said, "Okay, we're going to flip for the ownership of the airplane. Instead of all three of us, one of us will own it and can decide what to do with it."

I won the toss, and it was my plane. They got in their police car and drove away. Just like that. I had that Piper for a number of years and used it for my next business venture, my short stint as a prospector.

Drilling for Uranium

In 1946, the U.S. established the Atomic Energy Act, with the goal of managing and developing nuclear weaponry and nuclear power under civilian control. It was the Cold War, and nuclear power was viewed as the next great, efficient power source. So, the U.S. Atomic Energy Commission established itself as the only legal buyer of uranium in the U.S. and raised the price of uranium to create incentives for independent prospectors. It was the new Gold Rush. A fellow named Charles Steen, "the Uranium King" had become a multi-millionaire with his claim in Moab in 1952.

Uranium miners, 1953

There were articles and advertisements about him and about uranium prospecting in magazines and newspapers. A couple of neighbor buddies got very excited about this get-rich-quick scheme and convinced me to go in with them.

They staked our claim. We just needed a drill. None of us had much money, but I had the most collateral, so I borrowed $200 from the bank to buy the drill. Then I flew my two friends and the drill into Canada. They figured the Four Corners area of the Northwest would be mined out, but Canada, whose ban on prospecting uranium was lifted in 1947, was the new hot spot and where we'd make our fortune.

When we arrived, we had to wait until the next day to get to the site. It required a hike into this remote location, carrying the heavy drill.

"This is it," one friend said when we arrived at the spot, and we immediately went to work, looking for uranium. We camped and drilled for several days—and found nothing.

We headed home and never did go back or use that drill again. It sat on the floor of the garage at the 1021 W. Queen house for years and as of the writing of this book, may still sit on the floor of our garage in Santa Rosa. We were young. It was worth a try!

In the Dog House, 1957

By 1957, Bob and I had become partners in Harry's Market, and we opened a second location in the building adjacent to my house at 1005 Queen Avenue at the corner of Queen and Elm in a shared storefront with Cecil's Market.

Life continued to revolve around our family butcher shop business. My mom still did the accounts for both markets. I hand-painted signs for the day's specials, always trying to be very neat. The kids visited the store, getting to see their grandparents often and even helping out a little. My mom let Chris add up the charges for customers, obviously checking the addition. Sometimes, the kids

snuck to the back door of the market to ask for treats, like a fresh wiener from Nebergalls. Chris came so often that she became known as "Christeeny Weenie."

When we acquired the new shop, I also took over the lease of a small restaurant in a portion of the same building, a hamburger joint that catered to high school kids, since they would walk by on their way to and from school.

Originally called The Hideaway, we called it the Dog House in honor of the Albany Bulldogs. It had a juke box and an area for dancing and served milk shakes and burgers. You could get a hamburger at the Dog House for twenty cents apiece.

Bill Mikkelson, Meats

Bill has been associated with Harry's Market for over 10 years, serving you with tender, quality meats at low prices. Bill will manage the new market to bring you the same quality as Harry's Market has always offered.

My kids liked to come into the Dog House. When no one was watching, Bobbie, ten years old then, liked to dip her finger in the hot fudge container for a taste.

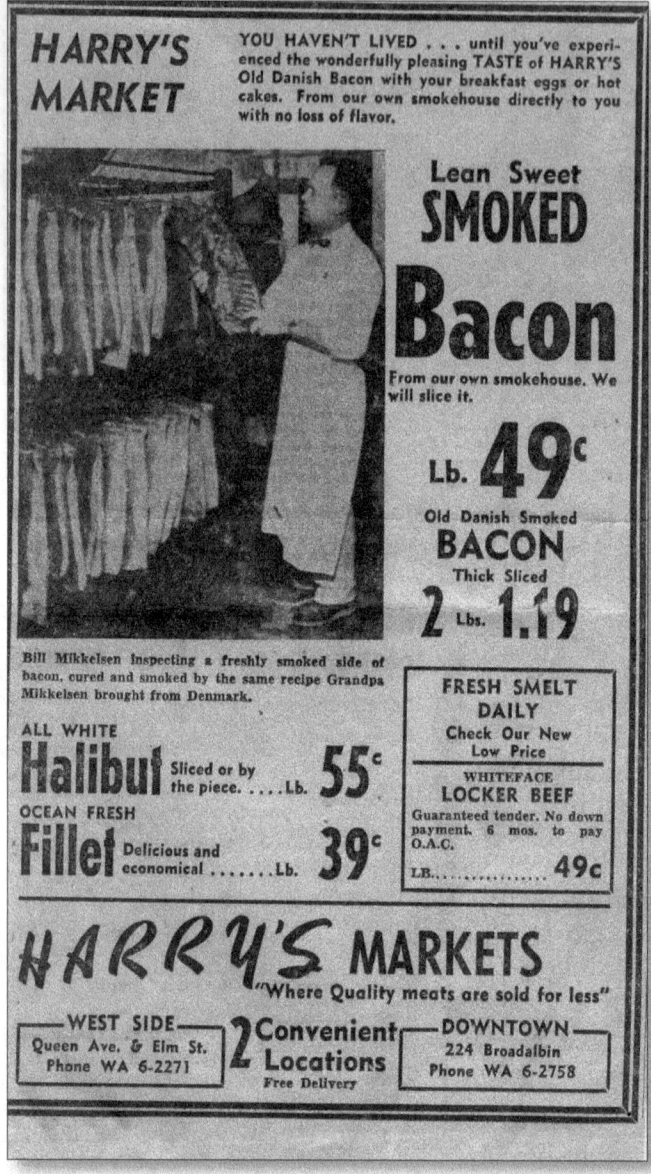

Chris, about eight years old, loved to watch the teenagers, boys who dressed like Elvis and girls with their rolled, long flip hairstyles. They'd play "Moon River" on the juke box, enjoying how the sounds drifted out onto the sidewalks. Sometimes on a particularly busy night, Fern would send the girls to get burgers and shakes for dinner. It cost one dollar to feed all five kids hamburgers, about another fifty cents for the shakes. Fern got skilled at making the milkshakes, which used real milk and ice cream.

The restaurant, however, did not turn a worthwhile profit, so I didn't keep it for long.

Chris trying out her "big kid" bike in front of our house, the Hideaway—the Dog House for a time—and Cecil's market in the background, 1955

Nutri-Bio

I was still looking for more income in 1957 when Nutri-Bio came on the market, selling vitamin, mineral, and protein dietary food supplements. The Nutri-Bio company marketed itself into a "national mania" growing to 115,000 distributors in the U.S. and Canada. Many people became wealthy selling the products, which seemed like good ones to me. I was always concerned with good health and being strong. So, I became a distributor, peddling the vitamins to as many of my friends as possible. But, that petered out pretty quickly.

Smoking Turkeys, a Danish Inheritance

As a meat cutter and partner in Harry's Market in the 1950s, I started smoking turkeys for our customers, with the bulk of sales being, of course, around the holidays. Smoked turkeys seemed kind of glamorous to our clientele. Of course, smoked meats were nothing new to the Mikkelsons.

My grandfather Mike brought the Danish practice of smoking meats with him from Denmark. With so many cold winter months in that far north Scandinavian country when hunting, fishing or keeping livestock was difficult, it was necessary to smoke or dry meats for protein. Smoked bacon, eel, oysters, and fish, including salmon, herring and halibut have long been Danish standard fare. My grandfather taught my father how to smoke meats, and my father taught me. And it turned out that this inheritance was valuable.

When I started advertising our smoked turkeys in local papers in the 1950s, they sold out, and every year, the demand increased. The success of these sales spurred an idea: If smoked turkeys were popular in my town, why wouldn't they be popular elsewhere? It had become clear from all my endeavors thus far that I needed a business that expanded way beyond Albany. Running a small local business was confining, physically, mentally and economically, relying on only a small community.

So, in 1957, with Fern's help, I started offering whole and half smoked turkeys not just around town but also by mail order. We called our business Danish Mikkelsons.

We acquired lists from and sold the meat through the Bear Creek Orchard in Medford, Oregon, better known under their marketing brand, Harry & David's.

Harry & David's, along with Pepperidge Farm out of Connecticut, both founded in the late 1930s, were helping to grow the specialty foods and gift mail order business, which boomed in the early 1960s. The timing was good.

I hired another meat cutter for Harry's, while I spent much of my time in the holiday months before Thanksgiving and Christmas, in the small smokehouse we built behind the store on Queen, a shack basically, where the smoking of the bacon and sausage for the store took place. Our little smoke house was only about a 10 x 10 brick building in which you could build a fire to create the smoke. We had rails on the ceiling from which we hung the raw beef and other meats and grilling racks for laying out other meats, including the turkey. To create the perfect turkey, the birds required a minimum of 36 hours basking in smoke made from a special combination of woods, plus other tricks of the trade.

As demand continued to grow, we rented a space at Fourth Avenue and Ferry Street to prepare the meat. We did okay the first year and by the following holiday season had orders for several thousand birds. We were fortunate. The Swift Meat Company was located nearby and had a lot of turkeys it couldn't sell. They practically gave them to us for how little we paid for them.

This business had potential, I realized. This could be big!

Sporting a new look in the late 1950s

Chapter Seven

The Smoke-Craft Years 1958 to 1976

IN 1958, BOB BECAME THE OWNER AND UNDERWRITER for Guarantee Mutual Life Insurance Company and was vice president and director of the First Federal Savings and Loan Association, making him a silent partner in Harry's Market. I still managed the store on Queen and Elm while my dad managed the store on Broadalbin, but I was spending more and more time in the smokehouse.

Smoke-Craft is Born

In 1958, I got a loan to buy another smoked turkey business belonging to Bill and Bernice Chase of Aurora. With this buy-out, came a large turkey smoking contract from the U.S. Navy, but we didn't have a plant in which to process the turkeys, let alone a plant that was approved by the federal government, which was needed in order to ship products between states. We had to move fast.

I financed and leased and redesigned a plant in Salem, Oregon, about 40,000 square feet or something like that, to kill the turkeys and ship them. We rented space for a bigger smokehouse locally at Second Avenue and Ferry Street, where the old Steen Brothers Market used to be. The company went from two (Fern and me) to about 20 employees.

I worked at Harry's during the day. In the evening, I went to the Ferry Street smokehouse. My cousin, Myles Ludwig became the plant manager and my business partner. Being an only child on my mother's side, my father first brought Myles on at Harry's. Just like with the crop-dusting business, I needed someone in operations, because I still had to manage Harry's Market and other aspects of this new enterprise.

The turkeys arrived in July. We slaughtered and cleaned the birds, smoked and packaged them and delivered them by the deadline of October 15th. I think seeing that truckload of smoked turkeys leave the plant was one of the greatest thrills of my business career up to that point. Our birds graced Thanksgiving tables all over the country for servicemen and civilians alike and their families.

We were becoming big enough that we needed a better company name. We had a contest amongst the employees to come up with a name people would remember. One of them invented the name Smoke-Craft and won the contest. The official start of the Smoke-Craft company was thus in 1959.

During the next couple years, I worked to remove the seasonality of the business by making turkey breast into jerky. It had a nice ring to it,

Turkey Jerky, and no one else offered it. I got the patent on turkey jerky, but I never reaped any benefit from the patent specifically. It just kept other people from using it for a short while. Turkey jerky naturally led into making beef jerky, which became much more popular than the turkey.

Making Jerky

Making jerky was a tricky business, given the specifics of the meat necessary and the meticulous process to create the final product. You need the meat lean, only the breast of the turkey and the top and bottom rounds of beef. That's the only part of a cow or steer that does not have any sinew or fat running through it. The meat must be salted to keep away bacteria. Then you marinate the meat, adding all kinds of rubs and spices or marinades to flavor the meat. This has to be tested to get the flavors you want, flavors people like.

Then you slice the meat into thin strips and hang them in the smokehouse to dry. You smoke the meat and dry them again. And then again. Smoke and dry. Smoke and dry. After that, you take them down, cool them and package them. We made our jerky in flat strips and sold it in glass jars. That was the first packaging, with forty pieces in each with our label on it.

We brought in the entire family to work at the business. Myles' wife Roberta helped make the jerky. Fern, all five of my kids, and Myles' four daughters helped pack gift boxes and tie bows and fill mail orders, putting in long hours during the busy holiday times.

We also smoked and seasoned other meats, making Landjäger (smoked Danish sausage), pepperoni, Polish sausage, peppered beef, and smoked chicken. Cousin Myles also knew how to smoke these meats, having worked as a meat cutter at Harry's for years. Bear Creek Orchards was interested in these too, and slowly, our products started to sell year around. People really seemed to like them.

Flying High

Reno Getaways

Another getaway to the World's Fair in Settle, Washington, 1962

With all my time away from the house working and traveling and skiing when I could, and Fern running the house with five kids, she occasionally needed a break. And deserved it! We were fortunate to have both sets of grandparents living in Albany, babysitters readily available. Reno, Nevada, turned out to be a great destination for an inexpensive weekend getaway, where we could fly to in my plane, and where we could relax and go out for meals and a show. We probably made our first trip to Reno in 1958. These trips were good for both of us to stay connected.

Camping with the Family

Of course, working six days a week made family vacations difficult, but making time for them were very important. Starting in the summer of 1959, Fern and I took our kids camping for two or three weeks a few years in a row at Jessie M. Honeyman Memorial State Park near Florence, Oregon, on Cleawox Lake, adjacent to the dunes, and about two miles from the beach. With facilities built by the CCC in the 1930s and a new campground added in the mid-1950s with electricity, water and hot showers, it was a great and easy place for families to overnight camp. A 1950s *LIFE* magazine even named Honeyman one of the Top 10 state parks in the nation because of all the activities and facilities there. For us, it was an inexpensive, fun and active vacation for a family of seven during those busy, lean years.

We would arrive at Honeyman on a weekend and stay in a tent and small house trailer. Another family usually joined us, towing a waterski boat to the lake. The kids loved playing in the huge sand dunes. We swam and boated and waterskied and had a great time. I returned to Albany to work during the week and then would rejoin the family at Honeyman for the weekend again before heading home. One of the families that joined us one summer vacation was the Barnes family from Albany. Mike later married Melissa Barnes, so our relationship with them continues today.

Fun Gliding on Water

Honeyman is where I first taught Chris to waterski. When they were old enough, I taught all the kids to waterski at one time or another, but that was nothing. I'd just get them up on a pair of skis, show them how to let the speed of the boat bring them up, and give them a good chance to get used to it. Then I'd show them how to release one ski and slip into a single, then how to get up on a single, then how to jump over wakes and so forth progressively. It was fun to see them improve and learn to do more. The kids say I was very patient, but I didn't mind circling around again and again if they fell in the water. It was fun to watch them get back up and try again. It was fun just being with the family on the water.

Skiing at Honeyman, circa 1960

I was in high school when I first learned to waterski, introduced to it by a friend who moved to Albany, Oregon, from Florida. He had waterskied all the time down there and told me about the weather and water off the southern coastline, which influenced my attraction to Florida later in life. Fern and I experienced it for ourselves at the end of my naval aviation training, and then later, Mike and his family settled there. During my Naval training and very early family years, I only waterskied now and then without much time for it.

Then, in the 1950s, friends re-introduced me to waterskiing on the Willamette River and Triangle Lake, about a one-hour drive from Albany. My friend Harold Fife and I decided to buy a used boat together. To this day, Bobbie and Chris recall those early waterski outings, sitting on the gravel bank of the Willamette on warm summer days. We'd bring a cooler with cold beer and soft drinks for the kids. One time when Bobbie was about 12 years old, in our enthusiasm, we forgot the soft drinks, having only packed beer. She let me know she was very thirsty! I felt pretty bad about that.

More Jerky, Less Harry's

Very few people in those days had even heard of jerky, so it was a new market in 1959, which made it risky but with grand possibilities. Our work was to get the word out, create a larger demand, and then keep up with production and distribution.

With the booming start of Smoke-Craft in 1959, by the end of 1960, we gave up the original Harry's Market at 224 Broadalbin where I cleaned the glass at seven years old and plucked chickens and spent most of my life. It became George's Fine Meats. My father became a silent partner, while I became owner of Harry's Market on Queen Avenue.

A friend of mine owned the McDonald Candy Company, and he became our first distributor of Smoke-Craft products. He had his own trucks and drivers and, besides candy, sold and delivered beer and glasses and other bar supplies to taverns and restaurants all around the state. He got my jerky into bars in every city in Oregon. It became popular quickly, a healthy snack food that went well with pub drinks. Everybody was just crazy about it. So, with the marketplace confirmed, we took the gamble further. Myles and I both borrowed money and mortgaged everything to grow what was then Albany Smoke-Craft Inc. I also needed other sources of income.

Pedaling my wares, early 1960s

A Laundromat & Duplex

So, I still kept up other enterprises. The Dog House had not been successful, but in 1961 I leased space around the corner from Harry's at 1620 Elm Street to try another venture, Mikkelson's Self-Serve Laundry. Coin-operated laundries seemed like a great business to me, requiring very little overhead to run. Fern helped out, taking on the responsibility of keeping the laundromat clean. The kids helped occasionally too with the daily collection of coins.

The girls remember emptying the machines, counting the coins and putting them in wrappers to take to the bank. The income from the laundromat was small but steady and helped cover the expense of the growing jerky business and our growing family.

I also came across the opportunity to purchase a duplex located on the next street over from our house, close enough to make management of it easy. You could see the duplex over our backyard fence. It was the first rental property I ever owned, and that was a good investment too.

Harry's Premium Food and Freezer Plan

Some of my business ideas required significant initial investment. But it was easier in those days. The folks in the bank knew me. I'd call them to tell them what I needed, go in at my convenience and sign the papers and get my loan. Wasn't that nice? I was always able to make the payments, so they liked me. This relationship came in handy with the start of new businesses and the growth of Smoke-Craft.

Also, in 1961 I launched another side business in an office next to the laundromat at 1610 Elm Street, Harry's Premium Food and Freezer Plan. Because of the butcher shop, I had access to stand-up freezers. The use of Freon for the consumer market had developed rapidly in the 1950s, outdating the old "icebox," but at that time, most people didn't yet have refrigerators with built-in freezer compartments, or if they did, the freezer area didn't hold anything larger than trays of ice. So, I saw a need for them. And of course, with access to both retail and wholesale foods, I could fill those freezers with quality meats and groceries, thus a "premium" food plan.

I went door-to-door in the evenings after our family dinner to show other families the advantage of having a home freezer. A stand-up freezer went for $1,800, and I made about $600 on every one I sold. Nowadays, of course, you can buy them for less than $200.

The food plan component especially seemed sound, being ongoing. This was long before Costco and that kind of thing made wholesale prices available to the everyday consumer. I hired a friend named HG Clyburn part-time to manage the company. He had a truck, so he could deliver the food to people for their freezers and cupboards.

That was not too much fun, having to hurry through my dinner with the family to get in the car and go out there to sell a freezer or two. But I sold my share of freezers and food plans and made quite a bit of money doing that. My oldest girls, Bobbie and Chris, needed braces, so I even traded a freezer to their orthodontist for teeth-straightening for both of them. That was a good deal.

Since I was already working full-time and had a family, however, it wasn't sustainable to go out every evening, so that didn't last too long. Besides, a new investment opportunity came along not long after.

State Savings and Loan, 1962

In 1957, my brother had become a director of the First Federal Savings and Loan Association of Albany. He and friends started the business and did very well and offered a valuable service. In 1962, two of my neighbors brought me in and said, "We want to start a business!" So, what did we do? We decided to open a savings and loan too. We called it State Savings and Loan. We flipped a coin to see who was going to be president. I didn't win. I got to be treasurer. We went out and sold stock with people investing $1,500 to $15,000 until we raised about $150,000. That wasn't very much money, but enough to get the permit, license and everything we needed to become a savings and loan.

We established a little office at 3rd and Broadalbin and opened the doors to State, which did well for 20 years. Over time, we opened branches all over Oregon and in California.

Our new home on Liberty Street, 1961

We were just under a billion dollars in deposits with seventeen buildings and one big headquarters in Albany when "the suits" came in during the 1980s. But it was great throughout the 1960s and the 1970s.

With all this, in 1961, Fern and I had the funds to build a beautiful new 3,700 square foot home surrounded by oak trees at 3240 S. Liberty Street. That became the kids' home for the rest of their time in school and Fern and mine well beyond.

Tennis & Albany Tennis Club 1962

Even with all these ventures and Smoke-Craft growing, I always made time for sports and physical fitness. It kept me going.

My neighbor and friend Bill O'Hearn introduced me to the game of tennis in the mid-1950s. I loved it, and it fit my lifestyle. You can complete a two-set match in an hour or less, getting a great workout and being social. I didn't play golf at that point. It took too much time away from the family and work. Also, the kids could play tennis. I taught all my kids how. Fern enjoyed it too. Like skiing, it was a sport we could enjoy as a family. I competed in weekend and evening tournaments, and Fern and I competed together in mixed doubles as well.

I played tennis almost every day before work or later in the evening after work when it was light enough.

At that time, the only accessible courts we had in Albany were a couple city courts at Henderson Park. So, a small group of us tennis enthusiasts began negotiations and plans to develop a tennis club. It was spearheaded by Bill O'Hearn, "Mr. Tennis," as we called him.

In 1962, we officially formed the Albany Tennis Club. We had the perfect spot for the club, the site of the original Albany College building on the edge of town (and close to our house) at W. 27th and S. Park Terrace (The college had moved to Portland and become Lewis and Clark College). Since 1938, the land had been owned by the Bureau of Mines. It was forty-six acres of bare land just sitting there. We tried to buy it from that government agency, tried and tried. We did not succeed.

In 1969 with ten families in our neighborhood committed to the project, we went ahead and built on the land anyway. We never even got title to it. We built two tennis courts to start with and became the charter membership of the Albany Tennis Club. It became a big place for the entire family to gather with neighbors and friends. We used the courts every day and invited other people to join the club outside of our neighborhood. It wasn't long before we added a swimming pool, two more outdoor courts, and a clubhouse locker room. Eventually the desire for year-round tennis brought the addition of indoor courts. And during all this building, we finally got the land.

The Albany Tennis Club has now been enjoyed by families for over 50 years. It had and still has a family-friendly atmosphere and is run by a dedicated and hardworking group of member owners, like the folks that started it. Our dog was even a member.

Champ, our spaniel, always followed Fern when she walked to the courts. Pets weren't allowed, but he'd stick his nose under the big wires of the fence and try to crawl under, staying right there outside the courts while she played, and then walking home with her afterwards. He was there so much, the Club's board made him an honorary member.

The kids probably enjoyed the pool most. We had issues with that pool though. One day, I was just about to serve in a singles match when I heard this strange, ominous sound, something large rumbling and moving. It came from the pool area. I went to investigate and discovered that the pool had come up out of the ground about a foot and a half. That may seem implausible, but it happened. The ground had gotten so wet from the rain that the swelling finally forced the pool up out of the earth. That presented a real problem. We had to either fix it or build a new pool. We did both, expanding the pool while addressing the issue so it wouldn't happen again.

Handball to Racquet Ball

In the 1960s, I got into handball as well. Handball, paddleball, racquetball, and squash all became increasingly popular in the 1960s, 1970s and early 1980s, and at some time or other, I tried them all (pickleball being the most recent addition to the set). Bill O'Hearn had a beautiful home in our neighborhood. At one point, he set up a handball court in his driveway, and I played with him there, usually on a break from work. We built the first handball courts at the Y in 1964, and then we played there often. My friend, Lee Walker, the manager of the YMCA with whom I played a lot, decided he was going to enter a handball tournament. He won, so he entered another. He won that one and entered another, until he became the world champion. That was exciting to watch.

When somebody loaned us some paddles, a half a dozen made of plywood, we turned it into a game of paddleball. In 1979, we built the new racquetball courts at the Y.

Spring Hill Country Club, 1963

In 1963, I lent a little labor to my friend Bud Fortier and his father Al who had built and opened the Spring Hill Golf and Country Club in Albany in 1961. We were among the charter members, even though I didn't play golf then. It started out as just a golf course with a small clubhouse that wasn't much more than an office. Bud was looking to greatly expand it and add a swimming pool. At his request, I joined the board and helped with fundraising and a membership drive, which succeeded to raise the money. I served as chairman of the board during the construction.

On May 30, 1963, we opened a two-and-a-half million-dollar clubhouse with men's and women's locker rooms, shower facilities, a pro shop, and eating facilities overlooking the pool, as well as a second nine. In April of 1964, Bud and Al handed over ownership to the members. The family enjoyed the pool there a lot too, but it wasn't until later that I actually had time for golf.

Jerky in the U.S.A.

Meanwhile, I spent long hours in the plant at 213 S. Ferry Street, serving as meat trimmer, floor sweeper, phone operator and bookkeeper, as well as salesman and spokesman. Whatever needed to be done, I did it. I worked a lot, but it never felt hard to me. Some people, and I'm one of them, love to work. It's just an appetite.

In 1963, Myles still helped run the business, and I hired Glenn Worden as secretary-treasurer. We were doing great business in the northwest, but I used the same line of thinking as before: if it worked here in Oregon, why not everywhere? It was time to go nationwide.

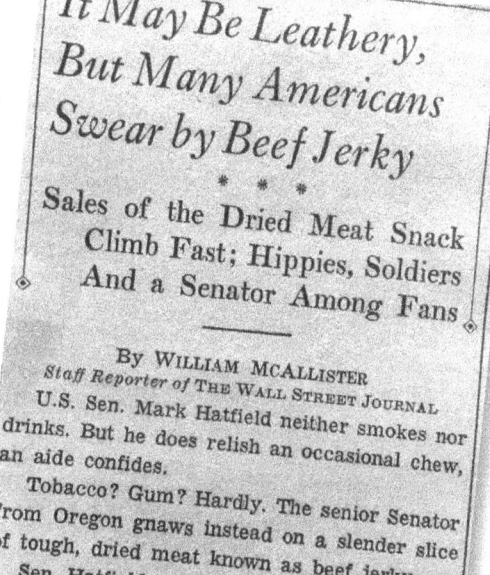

It May Be Leathery, But Many Americans Swear by Beef Jerky

* * *

Sales of the Dried Meat Snack Climb Fast; Hippies, Soldiers And a Senator Among Fans

By WILLIAM MCALLISTER
Staff Reporter of THE WALL STREET JOURNAL

U.S. Sen. Mark Hatfield neither smokes nor drinks. But he does relish an occasional chew, an aide confides.

Tobacco? Gum? Hardly. The senior Senator from Oregon gnaws instead on a slender slice of tough, dried meat known as beef jerky.

Sen. Hatfield isn't alone. Thanks partially to widespread use by GI's in Vietnam, beef jerky is becoming one of the nation's fastest growing snack foods. One industry source puts its retail

The Jerky Trip, 1963

That summer, I took the family on a country-wide camping and road trip that combined work and play. The "Jerky Trip" became a famous vacation in our family history.

I had it all planned out. We traveled a hundred or two hundred miles during the day to each destination, where we would set up camp early enough to have most of the daytime to play. I chose places where Fern and the kids and I could see a few sights or swim in a lake or play tennis or go horseback riding during the afternoon.

In our car and rented tent trailer were seven people, sporting equipment, clothes and swimsuits, camping supplies, and lots and lots of Smoke-Craft Jerky and pepperoni loosely in bulk. I couldn't bring it in its usual jars. You can't carry kids and all their gear as well as boxes upon boxes of jerky jars.

The camping was always fun. Mike, being the youngest and only boy, slept on the floor of the tent while the others had a mattress. I told them if they got up at night to go to the bathroom to be careful not to step on Mike's face. It became a running joke.

The family remembers it as a truly remarkable, memorable family adventure. The kids were thrilled seeing buffalo and bubbling lava pots at Yellowstone and awed at the sight of Mt. Rushmore. They were all frightened while sleeping on the second floor of my Aunt Clara and Aunt Mabel's home in St. Paul, Minnesota, when the loudest thunder any of us had ever heard literally rocked the house (Oregon has very few thunder storms). St. Paul was also their first exposure to humidity and fireflies.

Each evening after dinner, I would visit the bars and taverns in the area, dropping off samples of our jerky and promoting my products. I'd visit at least three bars in every town, seeking out the most popular. To find the three bars to go to, I'd strike up conversations with locals and ask which are the best bars in town. I gave each bar a free pack of jerky.

Fern with our camper and station wagon on the Jerky Trip, 1963

"See if your customers like it," I told them.

"Where can I get it?" the bar owners would ask.

In order for the bars to get the jerky, I had to find a local distributor. The way the industry worked: there were the bars and there were the local distributors of all the supplies to the bars. The distributor was my customer. He had the cash. So, I had to find the best distributor in each area, prove there was a market of interested bars, and provide the distribution company with the name of bar owners so they could order Smoke-Craft products from them. When the best bars in town offered our jerky and it sold well, the other bars would copy them.

I must've hit 50 bars or more during that three-week road trip around the U.S. And it worked. We were the first company ever to market the product nationwide. Beef jerky—and turkey jerky to some extent—was becoming a popular American snack food.

Building a Jerky Factory

By July 1963, I needed a factory to make my jerky. Myles and I found a property to purchase in south Albany at 850 SW 30th Avenue. I needed $150,000 to get it, a pretty big number. But with the aid of a loan from the federal government's Small Business Administration, I got it.

I needed someone to oversee the construction and then manage the factory. Glen Worden, or Big Glen as we called him, moved into that position. He was 6'4 and 270 pounds. Later, we hired Glen Pearson as assistant manager, who we nicknamed Little Glen, since he was as short as Big Glen was tall. We had a lot of fun with that. At the time, Glen Worden was a single guy living in the St. Francis Hotel, but with his hard work, he moved up in the world as Smoke-Craft did.

The completed plant when we moved in was about 10,000 square feet, not that big, but big for a little town like Albany. It was likely the only one of its kind in the nation at the time: a plant built specifically for the processing of beef and turkey jerky.

Within a short time, I was back at the bank getting a loan for another 50K to build an add-on to the factory. We were growing fast. Luckily, I had a good record with the bank and was able to service the debt because of what I invested in Smoke-Craft and my other businesses.

But it was nerve-wracking for a while. During construction, money was going out like leaves in autumn. I'd go to the bank and borrow the money we needed, and out it went. I'd borrow it again, and it was spent almost immediately. I have to admit, the high loan payments nearly caused me to throw in the towel.

But in general, I didn't worried too much about finances. There were, of course, problems because money doesn't grow on trees, and nobody gives it to you. You have to earn it and barter with the bank for loans and interest rates, but that was my job as Founder, and it was pretty exciting expanding into a big factory even though it took a couple of years.

Smoke-Craft smoked turkeys are in demand throughout the country. They're also a treat in the Mikkelson home, evidenced by Jennifer, 8, and Mike, 7, as they await a snack.

Smoked Turkeys Go Nationwide on Old Family Recipe

When Bill Mikkelson received his legacy, the occasion required no attorneys, no bankers—not even a notary public. His father simply taught him how to smoke.

The Mikkelson kind of smoking, however, is a habit other people get, and it's proving to be an inheritance every bit as valuable as a sackful of family jewels.

Recipe Handed Down

Generations ago, a Mikkelson ancestor in Denmark began smoking meat. The Mikkelson method had become a virtual art by the time it came to the United States with Bill's grandfather. In due time, the family secrets were handed down to Bill.

His contribution to the family tradition was the successful adaptation of the high-quality, slow-smoking formula to production in quantity. Thus was born Smoke-Craft, Inc., and from the firm's spacious and spotless new plant in Albany, Oregon, flows an imaginative assortment of both new and traditional products.

Slow Smoking

Smoked turkey is a time-tested Mikkelson product now being shipped on a mail order basis throughout the United States as well as abroad. The succulent, golden-brown birds — all broad-breasted Oregon turkeys — are the result of a minimum 36 hours of smoking, plus other tricks of the trade that Mikkelson isn't about to divulge.

Smoke-Craft's biggest run on smoked turkeys — as well as the firm's smoked chicken—is in the late fall and early winter season as holiday gift-givers and party-throwers swell the demand. Smoke-Craft birds grace many a Thanksgiving table over the country, too.

Smoke-Craft produces a wide range of smoked and seasoned meat products, including such delicacies as jerky (both the beef variety and the firm's "Turkey Jerky"), Landjaeger (smoked Danish sausage), pepperoni, Polish sausage and peppered beef. All are in growing demand in grocery stores and beverage establishments. They're also available by mail order.

Mikkelson doesn't mind jokes about his inheritance "going up in smoke," and neither do the 42 employees who profit by Smoke-Craft's progress. And there's another advantage to this sort of legacy.

"No inheritance tax," Mikkelson points out.

The smoking formula is as old as the Danish hills, but equipment in the Smoke-Craft plant is ultra-modern. Here, plump turkeys enter stainless steel smoke ovens—electrically-controlled, as is equipment throughout

the plant—where they will bask 36 hours in smoke from special combination of woods. (Right) Bill Mikkelson's broad smile means business is good as he displays part of Smoke-Craft's product array.

From the *Pacific Powerland* Newsletter, October 1963. It was an exciting time!

At the end, the Smoke-Craft headquarters was a beautiful two-story brick building with multiple stainless-steel ovens and lots of rails for hanging the meat to dry and smoke and then to cool. It was a long way from that little 10x10 smokehouse!

Jerky Around the Globe

We made Big Glen a minor partner in Smoke-Craft. He and Little Glen took care of all operations in our new headquarters in which we could now produce enough jerky to send truckloads out everywhere across the country and even ship it out of the country. They had the innate experience to make that all happen. Big Glen and Little Glen were a real good team, and I backed them. They hired and fired people, but mostly hired as we continued to grow, moving up to about 42 employees when we first moved into the building, then as the facilities grew 70, then 100 and more.

We had some good people too, and those good people attracted other good people. A lot of ladies worked at Smoke-Craft. The ladies tended to be very loyal to the company, as much or more than a man. If a woman was working in those days, she was unique. And we made it a habit to treat all our hard-working employees with respect. The employees knew me by name, and I would go around and say hi once in a while. That was a good relationship, which helped. If we were really busy trying to meet orders, there would be three shifts, and employees would work all night with Big Glen and Little Glen running the show.

Simultaneously, I owned Harry's Market, though I was no longer involved in its day-to-day operations, and it came time to let it go. The year 1965 was Harry's Market's final year in operation. The storefront on Queen Avenue became part of Cecil's Market.

After that, it was Smoke-Craft all the way. While the Glens kept the place running, my years from then on were filled with mostly marketing and sales calls. I was on the phone in touch with customers all the time or seeing them in person. By the late 1960s, we had sales all over the world, not just the United States.

I also did the buying of the meat. That was very important.

Around the World for Top Round

All throughout the 1960s, I searched the world for the best meat at the best prices. That was challenging. I would've loved to have bought American meat, but most ranchers in the U.S. did not specialize in the lean meat jerky required. It was too fatty. You can't smoke fatty meat, because the fat goes rancid. Being scarce, American lean meat was also much more expensive than imported lean meat. I had to look hard, but I found sources.

Most of our meat came from Australia. Several times, I traveled to Australia to the abattoirs (slaughterhouses) where they killed the animals and chilled them, and I handpicked the rounds I wanted. Each piece weighed about eight pounds. They'd put them in boxes, sixty pounds in each, and ship a boatload of that to Oregon in a freezer container.

On one trip in 1971, I donned an apron and butcher knife to show them how I wanted the beef orders cut. Evidently, they were impressed that the founder came instead of a company representative and doubly so when I was hands-on, reliving my butcher roots. I consulted with 18 different meat packing houses in Australia on that trip. The Australian Meat Board listed Smoke-Craft as one of 60 firms permitted to buy meat for direct importation to the United States. This was great, because in the past, we had to use a broker.

Throughout the years, I visited different locations in South America as well, including a 20,000-acre ranch in Columbia. I had to find suppliers in other countries because Australia's import quota limited us to one million tons of beef per year.

It was quite a journey to get to Columbia. I flew my own plane to La Manzanilla, Mexico, then from there took a commercial flight via Argentine Airlines to Bogota, Colombia. The owner arranged for a Piper to take me to La Gloria, then we drove by jeep the last fifteen miles to the ranch, which was in the middle of the jungle.

The cattle wandered free-range through the thick stands of trees. The ranchers didn't have a plant. To harvest the meat, they would kill the animals on the spot. I stayed with the ranch owner, Carlos Marulandia. Overall, it was an interesting experience but not a very good source for meat in the end. I imported a couple of loads, and that was all.

It was ongoing throughout the Smoke-Craft years, my search for range cattle producing lean round. I traveled to Mexico, New Zealand, and even Ireland once to find meat.

Family Trip to Hawaii, 1965

I was working 12 to 17 hours a day all during the Smoke-Craft years, traveling a lot and enjoying what I was doing. It was fun to watch the company grow. Still with all that, family was the most important aspect of my life, so I tried to be observant and present as a dad whenever I could. I was very grateful to Fern and her role as the main caregiver at home. She excelled at it. But it's important to be mindful. I kept trying to learn in that regard.

In about 1965, while sitting at the Thanksgiving table, with Oregon rain pouring down outside for the umpteenth day in a row, I looked at the family and decided we should go to Hawaii for Christmas. We had never been there. I called and told the airlines we had a "group," since there were seven of us, so we received group rates on a flight and hotel in Kauai. We had a wonderful time playing in the water and on the beach.

We were on a budget, so we all shared one hotel room. Without enough beds for everyone, Mike had to sleep on the carpet. That running joke from the jerky camping trip resurfaced. We all kept saying, "If you have to go to the bathroom, don't step on Mike's face!"

We were having so much fun that we missed the flight home, so they put the whole family in first class going back to Oregon. Such a treat for all of us.

Being a Dad During the Smoke-Craft Years

In the early years of the company, I enjoyed interviewing my children each evening, inquiring, "Well, how was your day?" My children were interesting. I would listen and be entertained for hours. I enjoyed playing with them and making them laugh. They're awfully good to me now.

It was great raising the kids in a small town where they had, between Fern and me, both sets of grandparents, three uncles, three aunts and six cousins.

My family with two sets of grandparents, 1963

With our many activities, this photo was taken for the local paper, 1960

All the kids showed maturity as they grew into adolescents and young adults. Bobbie and Chris, of course, being the oldest, were the first to go off to college, creating rich lives of their own. Both were at Oregon State University. Gail went to University of Oregon.

Being the youngest, Jennifer and Mike were home the most during the Smoke-Craft years, attending junior high and high school. They also grew up well, achieving many things. Jennifer was very active in her school. Mike was playing baseball, and I managed to go to a lot of his games.

The kids did all their studying for school independently and did well. Fern and I just encouraged them as best we could and sent them off to college. Paying tuition wasn't that big a deal in those days. All five could go. For the first couple, we did rely on some financial aid, but it was never a question. They were all going to get a college degree.

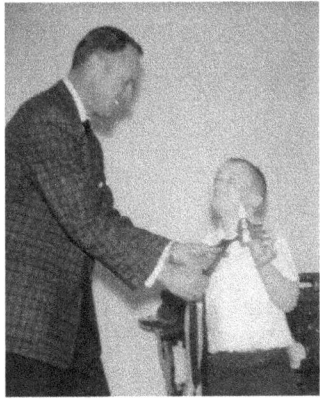

(Above) With my girls and Champ and helping Mike with his tie, 1962

(Below) Coaching Mike's little league team, 1967. Mike is standing far left.

Jennifer, Gail, Chris, Bobbie, Fern, Yours Truly, and Mike, Christmas, 1965

Bob, my mom and dad, and me, Christmas, 1965

Dad's weekend at OSU, Chris and Bobbie, 1967

Going Public, 1968

Just as quickly as the kids were growing and changing, so was Smoke-Craft. In December 1968, the company went public. We had our first stock issue at that time (and didn't have another for some time).

Serving on the nine-member board of directors were my brother Bob, and friends Rex Casey and William Scharpf among others. During one board meeting, one of them said, "You're not taking a big salary, Bill." Salaries at other companies they told me were twice what I was taking a year for the president. That was okay with me. But my brother and his friend on the board both suggested strongly that I take more. I thought it was kind of selfish. I didn't need it.

Becoming comfortable financially came gradually. In the early years as I said, the company kept needing more money to build a factory and then a bigger factory to substantiate the supply line. It took money to build a work force and infrastructure to increase the production levels. The ranchers were not going to cut up a cow just to take out one piece of round unless I made a commitment for a shipload of the stuff. I had truckloads coming in. I mean, big trucks.

We had our own trucks going out as well. As Smoke-Craft grew, we bought our own double-cab delivery truck and smaller trucks and hired drivers like Richard Owen, who took our packages of jerky and other meats up and down the coast and all around the nation. But the investment and hard work did pay off.

T and R Restaurant, 1969

During our major expansion in 1969 with Smoke-Craft doing so well, I thought of building more factories or a larger one. For that, I needed land. I wanted other avenues of distribution as well.

I found this restaurant for sale, T&R Truck Stop in Albany right on I-5 at the interchange with Highway 20. Interstate 5 was built a segment at a time through Oregon between 1957 and 1966 and had recently been completed. The entire stretch from Seattle to Los Angeles wouldn't be done until 1979. The restaurant's owners actually owned four different highway quadrants all along the interstate, 160 acres of land. The other three had nothing built on them yet. The owners had purchased the lots planning a chain of restaurants, but their circumstances changed and they needed to sell.

I bought the restaurant and the land through an exchange for 223,903 shares of Smoke-Craft stock. This made the deal tax-free. T&R was a huge restaurant-lounge and truck stop facility on 9.8 acres. It was open 24 hours a day, seven days a week, 365-days a year and was the biggest restaurant on the Pacific Coast at the time. It employed at least five head chefs, dozens of kitchen workers, two hundred waiters and waitresses, and an orchestra

every night. Being a truck stop, we had a shop with basic goods and a gas station as well as a parts and repair shop. We sold lots of tires!

Bud Fortier was in between jobs when I acquired the restaurant, no golf courses or anything, so I asked him if he would like to be manager. He did a marvelous job managing T&R for the entire time I owned it, from 1969 until 1976. Besides being a highly competent manager, Bud's a handsome guy and jovial, and just fun to be around. He's a people-person but also knew how to be the boss. With his leadership, I could pretty much stay out of the operation, and he made it successful.

We offered breakfast, lunch and dinner, but we especially liked to sell steaks because they were quick off the grill. They weren't as profitable, but they could be prepared and served quickly, leading to a larger volume of customers. T&R was a Greyhound stopover also. When the bus stopped there, forty-five people would get off and eat and be gone in an hour. We sold a lot of steaks at T&R!

The restaurant was making money, with net earnings of $45,914 and sales of $954,788 at the time of our acquisition. We increased this to over two million after our first year of ownership, so I kept it going and expanded it. The plan for the other locations was to build a string of franchised Smoke-Craft turkey restaurants.

A Big Sign

The sign when it was taken away

Such a big and profitable operation needed a big sign. We built, shipped by truck bed, and installed a sign that matched the establishment. It hung just about ten inches off the ground and went up forty feet and was about twenty feet across, wide enough so a disk jockey broadcasting there lived inside it for a week one time. It was that big! It had a toilet and bed and everything inside the sign.

I threw that all in when I sold Smoke-Craft, T&R and the land, which I never built on. But I didn't need to do that and felt afterwards I shouldn't have. It was a big corporation I sold it to. They managed T&R for a while and then—I don't know why—went and tore it down, the sign and everything. It's not there anymore. It's too bad. It would be fun to go back and eat there on occasion.

Becoming a Turkey Farmer

One of the reasons I wanted to build turkey dinner-type restaurants on the I-5 land was that in the couple years after acquiring T&R, I was faced with a surplus of turkey after the longtime threat of a shortage.

How to manage the supply of turkey for our jerky was an ongoing challenge. Only the breast was used to produce the final turkey jerky product and the huge residue of turkey carcasses became a disposal problem. You could say I had a hard time keeping abreast of everything! We countered this in two ways, by limiting the volume of the turkey jerky as we brought it into the marketplace and by getting a new space better equipped to handle the situation.

And I decided I'd raise turkeys to support the business and expand the volume of turkey jerky and smoked turkey.

In the summer of 1969, we acquired the Pilgrim Turkey Packers company. It came with a plant located on North Hyacinth Street in Salem, which we remodeled to become 32,000 square feet that November. It was basically a barn about a thousand feet long, more of a shed really. It also included 150 employees, which grew to 250 persons during peak periods. In addition, we bought the Mountain Park Farms of Redmond, which was equipped to raise 250,000 turkeys. We still had to purchase turkeys from independent mid-valley growers as well. Shortly after, we bought the Mt. Jefferson (turkey) Farms in Madras.

By 1970, we thus had two turkey farms and a processing plant for the birds, boosting our annual turkey population to 300,000. We were shooting for an eventual production capacity in excess of one million turkeys annually to support Smoke-Craft, T&R restaurant and possibly the franchised Smoke-Craft restaurants along I-5. For two years, I raised those little turkeys from eggs.

They say there's only one animal that's dumber than a turkey, and that's the guy who owns some! I discovered that soon enough.

New Products, New Production

By 1970, the Albany factory was 50,000 square feet with 125 employees. At its largest, Smoke-Craft employed around 200 people (not including T&R and the turkey plants). We were getting new business and reorders regularly. The growth of our work force and facility were key to meeting the wide distribution and making sure inventory shipped out on time, reliable production always the goal.

By October 1970, production was so big, we used the hindquarters of 275,000 beef, which added up to a lot of bull! We did our best to keep expanding our market and make jerky even more popular. I had to be careful not to sell more jerky than I could acquire meat for. We added products. Along with beef jerky, we made buffalo jerky. We also ran a smoked fish distributorship in Brownsville.

Our brand was fairly well-known by then, enough that I got a call from a businessman in Japan who was interested in bringing Smoke-Craft to their market.

Make No Little Plans

(A Quote on one of our YMCA fundraising campaign brochures that meant a lot to me.)

"Make no little plans. They have no magic to stir men's blood and probably themselves will not be realized. Make big plans. Aim high and hope and work, remembering that a noble, logical plan once recorded will never die, but long after we are gone, will be a living thing, asserting itself with growing insistence."

- Daniel Burnham,
American Architect and Urban Planner

Jerky in Japan, 1971

When I went into training for the war, it was against the "Japs." That's what we called them, purposefully labeled as the enemy, so we could do our job. They had snuck in and destroyed Pearl Harbor. I was known to have the best vision in my squadron during my training, able to spot their planes quickly and from far away for the purpose of shooting them out of the sky. Even though I never went into battle, I was well-trained.

After the war, I was aware that I had learned to hate the "Japs," characterizing them as killers. Well, it's not good to hold on to hate.

The Japanese trade organization Marubeni-iida Inc. had learned of Smoke-Craft and contacted me. They operated a large chain of neighborhood confectionary shops in Japan and had been studying the possibility of adding Smoke-Craft's snack food line at the stores. Another Japanese firm also proposed franchised production or a joint overseas marketing venture with Smoke-Craft and wanted to learn more about making and selling jerky in their country. I decided I would demonstrate to these Japanese businessmen that I could forgive them, that we could be partners. I agreed to go to Japan and talk with them, to help them in their endeavor.

I flew to Tokyo. This was part of a 27,000-mile, four-week business trip in January and February 1971 that included stops for meat in Australia, New Zealand, and Hong Kong as well.

One day during my time in Japan, I was presenting to eleven men. During the presentation, one by one, they got up and left, until none were there, leaving me in that room by myself for over an hour. It was very awkward and rude. Nonetheless, I didn't sever the relationship. They wanted help developing their own packaging, so I showed them ours.

I went home and then when I returned to Japan for a second time, I saw their packaging. They called their jerky something else, but otherwise imitated every last detail of our brand and package.

It looked exactly like a Smoke-Craft product without our brand nor a benefit to our company. At that point, I severed the relationship. That was an expensive lesson too, since I flew over there and back at my own expense. They didn't offer or give me a nickel. It was terrible.

I shared this story with another person in my industry, and he just nodded in understanding before telling me his story. He helped a Japanese company build a plant and do things to promote their products, thinking they had a partnership. He invested hundreds of thousands of dollars, and they walked off and left him. I came to understand that this didn't always happen between western and eastern partners. There were many successful partnerships as Japan "westernized" some of their practices and products. But unfortunately, it happened to me, leaving me with the impression that they were stealing ideas from the west. When I heard the jerky company in Japan went broke, I admit I was glad. It had been started dishonestly.

Black Butte Ranch 1971

In contrast to that unfortunate situation, we were doing well enough that in 1970 when two ski buddies suggested we invest in building a ski house at the newly developed Black Butte Ranch eight miles northwest of Sisters, we decided to invest.

I'd driven by that beautiful spot for years on the way to Hoodoo Ski Bowl or to Bend on business, admiring the beauty and location. It was a working ranch with a meadow full of cattle and the Three Sisters mountains as the backdrop. We decided on a lot on Fiddleneck Lane adjacent to the 7th hole of the new Black Butte Ranch golf course. I toured the land with the owner of the development. He showed me where we could build and where we couldn't. He said we couldn't build on the golf course. We went back and forth until he finally allowed us to build partially on the course, and we started into design and construction.

Smoke-Craft Years

The house was designed for the three families, with three main bedrooms upstairs, along with a family room and large kitchen. Downstairs was a big rec room and two more bedrooms, each containing bunk beds for four. There were five bathrooms. In theory, all three families could stay there together, but that never happened. Eventually one of the families built their own house at Black Butte. The other family divorced. So, I purchased the house from my partners.

The view was gorgeous in both summer and winter. For skiing, it was ideal, only 15 miles from Hoodoo and about 50 miles from the larger, developing Bachelor Butte, now known as Mt. Bachelor Ski Resort. During the summer, family, friends, tennis and golf buddies gathered there with Fern and me, sometimes for fundraising, sometimes just for fun. I auctioned off a week or long weekend there to raise money for the Y. Or people would come as our guests. I'd create mini tournaments for our tennis friends, with crazy, corny prizes. We'd give away a tricycle or even a little puppy. It was always fun. We made many treasured memories at Black Butte.

We continued to enjoy Black Butte Ranch for many years. Enjoying the hot tub with Carl and Barb Love, Fern, me, Vi, Bud Fortier, Bebe Barnes after a tennis invitational, 1985

Friends helped fix up the place too, with my favorite addition, a hot tub. One time, Fern and I were at Black Butte on our own, and we decided to get into the hot tub without our suits. It was a romantic, beautiful evening. When we were ready to go back inside the house, we found ourselves locked out! Wrapped in only towels, we started trying every door and window. Luck was with us when we found a small stained-glass window with a broken corner. It was just big enough for Fern's small hand to reach in and grab the knob to open the door.

Many swimming parties, barbeques, hiking adventures, bicycle rides and family adventures happened with Black Butte Ranch as the setting. When they were around four to six years old, I wanted to teach my grandkids how to play golf, so I cut down some clubs to their size and taught them to swing. I've always enjoyed teaching. It was fun to come up with new activities or locations to explore while we were there, taking in a new hike or horseback riding around Suttle Lake, for example. New ideas were always possible.

I kept an old car at the Sisters Airport so we could fly the thirty-minute flight from Salem to Black Butte. Any excuse to fly! That airport has a really short landing strip, and many times I had a rough landing, scaring whoever was flying with me.

Chris owns the Black Butte house now, so it's still in the family.

Big Glen and the Stock Fiasco, 1971

With the success came a couple major challenges to Smoke-Craft. In 1971, something strange was happening to our stock value causing it to go down. At first, I couldn't explain it. One of the stockholders complained to the media about the company's income descreasing. I was still taking a modest salary, $34,127 that year (equivalent to about $215,000 today). There were no top-heavy salaries or bonuses. As a matter of fact, our recent negotiations had deleted bonuses. I couldn't figure out what was going on. When I looked into it further, I found out the price of our stock was going down because someone was selling it. Then I found out who.

Little Glen never had any stock in the company, but Big Glen had about five or six percent. While at Smoke-Craft, at thirty-seven years of age, Big Glen married for the first time. His new wife was a blonde bombshell with a convertible who found him and basically said, "You will marry me." At least that was how it looked from the outside.

I guess he was happily married, but she insisted they buy a lot and start building her dream house, and unbeknownst to me, Big Glen sold shares of his Smoke-Craft stock to put money into that house. He didn't tell me what he was doing, and he was not supposed to be selling the stock.

I was quite resentful when I found out. Our stock value would go up four or five points and then drop back down again, over and over, like a yoyo. It affected the value of the company, shareholders' confidence, and it almost sank the company. Finally, Glen came clean, and we talked about it, but there was nothing I could do about the shares he had already sold and his trading's impact.

Smoke-Craft had become profitable by then, and I was paying the bank back with my share of the profit. I didn't sell any of my stock. I earned a salary and put money back into the business to grow it. It took some serious hard work to pull Smoke-Craft out of that fiasco. I guess Big Glen was happy in his new marriage, but his actions broke our trust and friendship. I fired him. I didn't forget all the good he did the company in the past, but I had to sever the relationship. Little Glen took over the management of the factory.

Then came another large problem that needed fixing. It was dumb. With feathers.

Dumber Than a Turkey...

The turkey farms were a bust! Our income in 1971-72 was depleted by losses suffered in our turkey operations. I sold them as quick as I could, and by 1972, I was out of the turkey farming business. There was also a water buffalo shortage during that time, and we had to drop that product too. We lost the Canadian market in the first quarter of 1971 due to new health rulings on the importation into Canada of smoke-dried products. For a while, I considered building a Canadian plant, but it didn't make sense financially.

Once all the "turkeys" were gone, however, we were able to really concentrate on production once more. With Bill Mitchell as vice president and general manager, we reached monthly sales of $1 million for the first time in July of 1972. Our newest smoked sausage snack, the "Hickory Stick," along with more sophisticated marketing strategies were significant factors. Smoke-Craft products by then were seen in supermarket outlets, outdoor stores, health food shops, sporting goods stores, specialty shops, and the taverns where it all started.

A fun marketing challenge I enjoyed was building jerky's reputation as a healthy sports snack.

Jerky and the Trail Blazers

As part of my efforts, I sponsored a Portland Trail Blazers game. The team joined the Western Conference of the National Basketball Association in 1970, and we sponsored them soon after.

I went to the basketball game and gave out samples of our high protein snack to everybody there, 17,000 people. Mike got to be a ball boy that night.

That was a pretty big night. They had us sit courtside, ushering us in. "Mr. and Mrs. Mikkelson, you're sitting over here," said our hostess, gesturing to our seats. And at half-time she reappeared, asking cordially, "Would you please stand and wave at the crowd?"

It was a costly marketing idea, but fun. The papers covered it, and it made for a memorable time. In 1976 Smoke-Craft sponsored the Blazers again and introduced a new rounded-shape hunk of jerky. It was called "The Trail Blazer." They won the national championship during the 1976-77 year, which was a huge event. The team awarded me a basketball signed by all the players as well as a silver cup. That was a treat.

Smoke-Craft Goes to the Olympics, 1972

More successful and widespread was our sponsoring of the U.S. Olympic ski team in the 1972 Winter Games in Sapporo, Japan. That was fun for me since I was a certified ski instructor and an avid skier. We went to Bend to meet the Olympic team and coaches when they were training. The first time I went, I missed them because they were off skiing somewhere else, but we returned. I asked the coaches if they would be interested in trying our product. This led to a meeting with a board member of the USSA (United States Ski Association) in Seattle, in which the Association agreed to endorse Smoke-Craft, and I agreed to do a special promotion with our products that would raise about $3,000 to send the team to Japan. I told them jerky is a quick energy, healthy pocket food, and every skier should have it.

That was in February. Until the end of March, we sent a full supply of jerky and other Smoke-Craft products to every Can-Am (Canadian-American) winter series skiing event, supporting all the competing skiers not just the Olympians, as well as their coaches and the officials on the mountain. There were cartons of Smoke-Craft beef jerky at the starting line of races. We added on our packaging "approved by the U.S. ski team," and a percentage of every package of jerky sold during the promotion period went to the Olympic team. Smoke-Craft jerky eventually went to Japan with those competing for medals.

This particular venture was a successful attempt to have consumers associate beef jerky with outdoor sports. Because jerky is light and nutritious, we were also able to get Smoke-Craft into the hands of climbers, who took the snack food with them on expeditions to the top of Mount McKinley and Mount Everest.

We were, by then, the world's largest supplier of jerky, even with competitors popping up on the scene. Our affiliation with athletes helped us stay on top of the market.

Hiking and Mountain Climbing

I did some hiking myself during these years. Ever since my scouting days as a boy, I enjoyed hiking, but it takes a lot of time, so during my working years, it generally only happened on the occasional weekend. Over time, however, I had the pleasure of climbing many of the Pacific Range mountains in Oregon. Five of them weren't far away and were the first I hiked—Mount Jefferson, Three Fingered Jack and all three of the mountains known as the Sisters. The person that got me started was my friend June Hauger. We skied together regularly. She was a very good skier and all-around athlete, one of the guys. She came walking by my house one day in the summer while I was out picking up the paper or something. She said, "How would you like to climb Three Fingered Jack?"

I said, "I'd love it."

"Well, a few of us are climbing it a week after next."

The morning before, she came by and said, "Well, it's tomorrow," just to remind me. Maybe she thought I'd back out.

It was an all-day climb, from morning to dusk, so we brought equipment to set up camp at the bottom of the mountain afterwards. With water, food and good walking shoes, off we went.

At the very top of Three Fingered Jack is a precipice only about five feet in diameter, built like many of the volcanic peaks in the area. You have to scramble up the rocks to get to the top, so it's okay going up, but going back down isn't all that much fun. Once on that tiny ledge with the wind blowing, I could sit down, but held on tight to the rocks around me, afraid to let go, because one step off the edge, and I would fall what appeared to be hundreds of feet onto rock. But the view was spectacular. We could see at least seventy-five miles in any direction that day. It felt like quite an accomplishment.

June was fearless. She stood right on the edge and twinkled her toes over the threshold. She turned around backwards, balancing her toes, moving her feet up and down over the expanse as if about to execute a back dive off a diving board. One slip and she'd be dead. But that didn't bother her. And as fellows might have said back then, she was "just a girl." She set the bar for me.

Another weekend, I started up one of the other mountains with six or seven others in the late afternoon. We brought camping gear, planning on spending the night at the top. It grew windy and cold as it grew dark, and I had to borrow a jacket from one of my friends. We finished the climb by moonlight and came back down the next morning. Climbing in the dark is a little spooky. Several people in the group stopped part way and turned around.

Fern was very understanding of my adventures. She thought some of them were foolish and a waste of time and would not do them herself, like climbing precarious mountain peaks. But she never tried to stop me. That's love! We spent a lot of time together and had quite a few wonderful, less harrowing adventures of our own.

Looking back now, I guess I was kind of a domineering husband at times. If I wanted to go somewhere, I would said, "We're going to go." To some of them, she might say, "Well, I don't think we should. I don't want to." I would retort with "None of that whining." And she went. Overall, she was willing and ready for a lot. For our ski trips and other travels with the family, she would pack up all the kids' things, take care of any food we needed, button up the house, and more. She had so much to do, but she was game for most of it. I'm grateful!

Other Travels During the Smoke-Craft Years

During the Smoke-Craft years, especially the early ones, I traveled mostly for business, but occasionally with Fern for pleasure, and with the kids, although the older ones were off in college, and it wasn't long before Jennifer and Mike were too, Jennifer to Seattle Pacific, a small, Christian private school, and Mike to Scottsdale Community College, concentrating on his baseball prospects before transferring to Linfield College, where he took business classes.

I did a lot of snow skiing in winter, and we waterskied on Lake Shasta in summer. I was fortunate. I always worked for myself, and I had people like Bud Fortier, Big Glen and Little Glen, and then Bill Mitchell looking after day-to-day operations, so I could get away.

Fern and I returned to Hawaii with friends and enjoyed it so much, we bought a timeshare on Maui. But it seemed like by the second time we used the

Back to Hawaii with the family: Jennifer, Bobbie, Mike, Chris, Fern, and Gail, circa 1974

timeshare, we got disenchanted. I tried and I tried to sell it while I was there, and I didn't succeed. So, eventually I put a note up on the bulletin board, and when I got

Skiing with the family, circa 1967

home, somebody called me and bought it. But we continued to travel to Hawaii in the late 70's and for years after.

Fern and I did have a big five-week trip to Europe in June 1970 while Chris was studying in Italy. We visited London, England; Paris, France; Rome, Florence, and Pavia where Chris lived and other cities in Italy, Switzerland, Austria, Germany, and Holland. We saw many famous sights, the Eiffel Tower, the Vatican, the Heidelberg Castle, Ann Franke's house and more and had some great experiences. We even played some tennis in Austria. We really caught the travel bug.

Service on the Side

All the while, I remained very involved in the community. Those were busy years, but going to church and supporting the Presbyterian Church were always a regular and important part of our lives. I got involved in a building campaign, helping to raise funds and pledges for a new educational wing of the church. I was active in Kiwanis Club still. I was chairman one year of the March of Dimes and chairman of the Albany United Fund Drive another (1964).

I took a turn serving as a board member of the Timer Carnival Association. I continually supported the YMCA, serving a term as president of the organization as well as the Albany Tennis Club, and in 1970 the Albany American Field Service unit. I also was active in the Elks, Masons and American Legion. This all meant that I had many meetings. The kids would ask Fern, "Where's Dad?" Her pat answer was: "He's at a meeting!"

Fern was also busy serving our community. She led March of Dimes campaigns, worked on Jaycee projects, and spent a lot of time as chairman of the Camp Fire Girls. Annually, we'd take the cars out of the garage and fill the space with candy for the Camp Fire Girls to sell. The girls sold a lot of candy and made a lot of money. That was quite an operation. In 1970, Fern was recognized

A NEW BRAND of candy, although still a mint is being sold by members of Camp Fire Girls Inc. this year. Eager to sell Brown and Haley chocolate covered mints are Bluebirds Nancy Govro and Kathleen Pharis. With the girls is Mrs. William Mikkelson, candy sale chairman for the third straight year in Linn and North Benton counties. The mints, which will be on sale for 10 days, beginning Friday, are being sold in all of the Willamette Council, including Polk, Marion and Yamhill counties.

for all her 13 years of service for the Camp Fire Girls and was presented with the highest-level award, the Luther Halsey Gulick Award, named for the organization's founder. She earned it! She also helped the Brownie Scouts, Rainbow Girls and was constantly sewing night gowns and dresses for herself and the kids. She was also excellent at decorating and maintaining our house. It always looked beautiful. So did Fern!

Helping to build a YMCA in Albany

My long career supporting the YMCA started and grew through the Smoke-Craft years. In 1958, four of us, my friend Bill O'Hearn being one, got together and said, "We should have a YMCA in Albany," most especially for our youth. Others helped and things moved quickly. By April 1959, we had an office for the Mid-Willamette Family YMCA and a campaign for membership. I was a founding member. By summer we had a manager. In 1960, we were able to acquire a building.

The front of one of our many fundraising brochures, 1967

> **Build Forever**
> (From inside a Y fundraising brochure)
>
> "Therefore, when we build, let us think that we build forever. Let it not be for present use alone; let it be such work as our descendants will thank us for, and let us think, as we lay stone on stone, that a time is to come when those stones will be held sacred because our hands have touched them, and that men will say that they look upon the labor and the wrought substance of them."
>
> - Ruskin

It wasn't too far from the Smoke-Craft plant, an old Howard Cooper farm implement factory, a big, ugly, two-story place with long areas of just plain concrete. It took a big fundraising campaign to remodel the building completely, putting in big windows, and digging a hole for a pool. We finally had our Albany YMCA! It was a walkable distance from my plant, so I went to the Y at lunch to play handball, go swimming, then return to work.

From them on, we kept raising money to add on and improve the Y. We had one big campaign in the early 1960s to build a new teen center and gymnasium. My brother and my friend Jim Goode served on the board with me then. Jim was a lawyer in town. At the writing of this book, he and his wife lived on the same block as Bud Fortier and came to visit every once in a while.

In 1966, I served as president of the board of directors at the Y and worked with a team on another major membership drive with a kick-off dinner at T&R restaurant.

My work with the Y never stopped. Even in 2013, there was a campaign. The director, who had just retired, was a friend of mine. We tore down the original farm implement place and built a brand-new facility. The current one is all new with big glass walls. We remodeled the old pool and built a second indoor swimming pool.

I stayed on the board on and off, but other than that one presidential year, I shoved the leadership off onto other people because they could do it better and had more time. Still, it was full-time work during major campaigns, a big part of my life. I'm sure it was a drag to my family, but it built something special for the community.

To this day, our club in Albany is known as the finest YMCA on the Pacific Coast, winning recognition for such. I worked hard for that. It's truly a nice heritage to have. They didn't name it after me though!

Skiing Fast at Shasta

Eventually, Fern and I started taking the kids for waterski vacations on Lake Shasta in Northern California, where we'd rent a houseboat and live on that for several days or a week, towing a speed boat along for daily waterskiing.

Good guy

To the Editor:

It would be greatly appreciated if you would publish the following letter regarding Mr. William L. Mikkelson, 3240 Liberty Street, Albany.

Few people would unhesitatingly loan their family car to four grubby-looking characters stranded on the side of a lonely country highway at night. But Bill Mikkelson did.

Mr. William L. Mikkelson (president of Smoke-Craft) not only did this, but he also hitched up our 14-foot boat and trailer to the back of his car and drove us all into Albany from just east of Newport. Since we live in Eugene, Mr. Mikkelson then insisted that we take his car home for the weekend and return it to him at our convenience after our own car had been repaired.

We just couldn't believe anyone could be quite so trusting and generous to four total strangers. The people of Albany certainly must be proud of this kind citizen and his family. How fortunate you are to have him.

Bill, Norma & Toni Manning
649 E. 16th Street
Eugene
Mrs. Francis D. Manning
1745 Lakeview Drive
Klamath Falls

I wanted to help theseee folks in any possible way. They were strangers, of course, but they were human beings. What did I care? I didn't care if they stole the car, wrecked it; it didn't make any difference to me as much as to help them. So that's what I did.

Our family got acquainted with other families on the lake in their rented houseboats, and we'd pull in next to one another on the banks. There, we'd swim, jumping off the boat in the water, share the speedboat, and spend the night sleeping under the stars.

Skiing every day for a week, I guess we thought we were pretty good. I'd ski on just my left ski, then just my right ski. We'd ski with the flotation belt tied around our waists. I really enjoyed it.

I think I was the only person in my family to be injured while waterskiing though.

When Michael was perhaps in his last year of high school in 1974, he asked me one summer evening if I would take him and two of his friends waterskiing after dinner. I said, "That's fine. Let's go."

It was a warm summer night with almost nobody else out on the lake. The water was warm, the sun was setting, and the surface of the lake looked like glass. I piloted the boat while the three young men took turns skiing. By then, it was getting pretty dark, but I loved skiing smooth water.

"How about taking the old man?" I asked.

One of the boys said, "Better slow it down."

I faced him and said, "Speed it up."

We were jockeying, of course, big smiles on our faces, and they did speed it up. They got me going around turns pretty darn fast, 40 or 50 miles per hour, enough to whip me around. Finally, on one turn, I took a spill. I cartwheeled four times over the water. When I felt horrible stabs of pain, I knew I was in pretty bad shape and for a moment thought, "Well, maybe this is it."

With my life vest on, I popped up on top of the water. The boat was gone, the boys not having noticed yet in the increasing darkness of night that I had fallen. I bobbed there by myself wondering what damage I had done until they came back. Adrenaline helped me get in the boat. When I went to the doctor, it turned out I had cracked three ribs. It was a humbling experience.

Mike continued to enjoy waterskiing as well and bought a boat of his own in Florida. When we visited him there in the 1980s and 1990s, I'd waterski, and it was in Florida in the 1990s that I waterskied for the last time.

Starting Self-Stor, 1972

After that one duplex, I acquired a couple of apartment rentals near the college. I was still trying to create other revenue streams, and it didn't take that much to purchase apartments at that time. Property was much less expensive than it became in the decades to follow.

In 1972, I was approached by a friend named Rocky Conser who had an idea for a business venture that sounded promising. Rocky and his brother also grew up in Albany. The idea was to purchase land near apartment buildings in college areas and build warehouses made up of many small, individual storage units and rent them out to people to store excess belongings. That sounded promising, and Rocky became my business partner.

Boy, there are tales about him! Rocky was supremely handsome and charming, great with the ladies, full of ideas but also full of himself. He was first married at 17 and a father at 18 and in his lifetime, was married and divorced three times. He loved the outdoors, and Fern and I traveled a couple times to Mini Storage Conventions with him and his wife at the time, Marilyn. He was a good businessman but could be a devious son of a gun too. He knew how to make money. Later on, after several years of being partners in storage units, we really came to loggerheads, but that story's yet to come.

Storing goods wasn't new, but the infrastructure was. People previously rented space in warehouses, where their things were labeled and shelved, sitting beside other people's things. That's how the storage industry looked for 100 years.

The idea of individual spaces that people could access almost any time, without the cataloguing necessary in a warehouse was absolutely new as an industry, a ground-breaking venture.

It was being done by companies on a small scale in Florida and Texas, but that was it. We called our business Self-Stor, which became one of the first self-serve storage facility chains in the United States.

Rocky and I formed a 50/50 venture with Rocky acting as the primary developer/manager while I put up the money. As president of Smoke-Craft, my interest in Self-Stor had to be somewhat passive, but I maintained an active role in decision making. We started in Albany in a building with about twenty-five units. They filled up quickly, so we acquired a little more adjacent land and added another ten units, then ten more. Pretty soon we had fifty units and then a hundred. With this success, we concurrently looked for other locations.

Expanding Self-Stor

Each property had to be near to apartment buildings or colleges where people were renting and had limited space. It helped if the building was quite visible and easily accessible. We expanded to Corvallis, Eugene, Salem, McMinnville, and Bend. Once we had the land, it didn't cost hardly anything to build the structures. They go up fast.

The business grew quickly, with the addition of three or four new locations each year. After four years, we ended up with twelve Self-Stor buildings around Oregon. It was very profitable.

Taking Over as Sole owner of Self-Stor, 1976

Over time, the business relationship with Rocky became, well, rocky. We had very different ethics, which does not work well in any partnership. He adulated on that, living a fast life, and a certain amount of drama. One time, he had me take his wife skiing. I don't remember much, but it was probably to teach her how since I was a ski instructor. Then he accused me of sleeping with her. It was crazy.

It turned out that he was not honest in business undertakings.

Finally, in 1976, I found out he had taken $150,000 off the top and put it in his name. That was it. I took him to court.

It was a challenging time in many respects. In the midst of our disagreement, we decided to turn over all the management functions of the storage business to Jack Gainer of ULI management services in Oregon. Jack's daughter, Lynn Mishler and a capable associate named Kevin Howard helped run the business.

The Self-Storage Industry

It's been said that approximately 6,000 years ago, the Chinese would often store their possessions in clay pots in public underground storage pits. America made it an industry.

In the 1850s, Bekins built warehouses for the storage of household goods and valuables. People were moving more frequently with westward expansion. With the industrial revolution, some families had more accumulated belongings than ever before. In 1906, Bekins built the first reinforced steel and concrete warehouse in Los Angeles, and the second in San Francisco, which withstood the great earthquake of 1906.

The Collum family is credited by some for the creation of the first modern self-storage facilities (like Self-Stor), which began to appear in 1958 in Fort Lauderdale, Florida. There are also claims that self-storage originated in Texas in the 1960's with the building of prefab, tin garage-like structures.

The big national players in the self-storage industry arrived on the scene in the early 1970's: Public Storage, Shurgard, and Storage USA. At the time this book was written in 2019, there were over 50,000 self-storage facilities in the United States with approximately 566 storage units per facility, a total of 2.3 billion square feet of rentable storage space. One in 10 people use self-storage in the U.S.

Soon after turning the management business over to ULI, we settled our lawsuit. We met up for a final showdown and he said, "I'll buy you out."

I listened and listened. When he was done, I said, "Why don't we just turn this around, and I buy you out?"

I was surprised that he agreed to it. Overnight, I became the sole owner of the business and in retrospect, it wasn't a lot that I paid him for his half. I got rid of my unwanted partner and owned all of these prospering self-storage units, operating the business using ULI as manager. We built even more, and my son Mike later became interested in the business. I was lucky.

Because I was in the self-storage business, I was a member of the Oregon Self Storage Association and the National Self Storage Organization, too. On occasion, I'd go to conferences and visit other self-storage companies and sites. I became pretty knowledgeable about the industry being among the originators.

Laundromats

I had another close friend who was well-to-do (having married into money), and he owned about a half a dozen self-serve laundries. I had done well with my single laundromat in town, so when he wanted to sell them to me, I said yes. That started my laundry chain. That business grew too. I did the same thing as with the Self-Storage units: I looked for promising locations and either bought an existing building or land to build a new laundry. We started in Oregon.

Scanning for locations in the various college towns became a convenient excuse to fly. I was lucky, I guess. Although I looked for opportunities as well and worked hard.

Selling Smoke-Craft to International Multifoods Corporation

And after seventeen years, I decided it was time to sell the jerky business. By 1976, the storage unit business was making more money than Smoke-Craft. Other food makers were offering jerky and looking to increase their market share. With a lot of help, I had grown a successful business, so large competing companies were making offers to buy me out, including General Mills.

Before I sold it, I offered the company to my son Mike. While he was at Linfield College in McMinnville playing football and taking business courses, we began to have some sincere discussions about his future occupation options, including taking over as head of Smoke-Craft. That summer, he traveled with the Smoke-Craft head of sales, Bill Mitchell and made some sales calls to check it out. My brother Bob was pursuing Mike as a possible associate in his Life Insurance/financial planning firm as well.

After a family trip to Hawaii for Christmas 1976, flying on New Year's Day, Mike joined me on a trip to Sydney, Australia. He came with me to meetings, and I arranged for him to work in the Tancred Brothers meat processing plant in Brisbane and live with the owner's family for a month.

That year, I got a call from the International Multifoods Corporation, which was one of the "Big Three" food makers in the world. Their brands included Stouffer's frozen dinners, Robin Hood flour, Kaukauna Klub cheeses, and Kretschmer wheat germ. Multifoods offered me a good price for the company.

I called Mike to tell him I was contemplating selling Smoke-Craft and asked him whether now he was interested taking over the company. I never wanted to pressure him. I wanted all my kids to follow their hearts. But the opportunity was there for him.

While I consulted with Multifoods, they still used our brand name and story.

Mike thought about it for a few days and called me. The meat business was not where his heart was. It wasn't long after that he found his calling in real estate.

Once I sold Smoke-Craft, that was it. The restaurant went with it, so did the factory and the tasting area connected to the factory, a little shop where people could go in and try jerky on site. With the merger, I signed a three-year employment contract with Multifoods as the manager. Myles was assistant manager. They were based in Minnesota. I was in Oregon. I don't remember if I even got paid anything, but I must have. I think I just had to sign that in order to complete the sale. We arranged for Multifoods to acquire the company in a tax-free exchange of stock that investment counselors said was advantageous to Smoke-Craft stockholders. About ten minutes after we merged, our stock was split two-for-one, which was a wonderful financial win for all involved.

I had given shares of Smoke-Craft stock to each of my kids so my ownership could be more than 50%. With the sale, they all reaped rewards, so that was good.

This brought me into early semi-retirement at age 55. It allowed me more time for myself and with my family, and traveling for pleasure, which, with an empty nest, Fern was ready and excited to do. I had never worked only a 40-hour week during that entire 20 years, so it was time to work less.

International Multifoods Corporation went on to sell the Smoke-Craft brand in 1986 to Curtice-Burns Foods, best known for Birds Eye brand, and then Curtice-Burns later acquired the Lowery's meat snack brand and combined the two into the Curtice-Burns meat snacks. In 1994, they sold both Smoke-Craft and Lowery's to Oberto Sausage, another Pacific Northwest company, which overnight made Oberto the largest jerky manufacturer in the world.

Visiting the Oberto plant, my old plant, in 1994

The Last Few Jerky Years

I did continue with business projects, overseeing Self-Stor (though not managing the day-to-day), working on building condominiums in Eugene. I even invested into a new aircraft design with a partner in Mesa, Arizona. The design was for a combination car and plane. That was a bust! But it was an exciting idea (Finally, in 2018, there were several designs out there that worked. Who knows! Maybe I'll still see them sold and used regularly in my lifetime.)

It was quite a transition from two decades of a very full work and family life. But we managed! All the children were off living lives of their own, some married. We even held our first grandchild, Aaron, (Chris and Rob's first), born September 11, 1977. I consulted with Multifoods about their new Smoke-Craft holding but had lots of time off. So, Fern and I started traveling more for pleasure.

Trips While with Multifoods

A few examples of our travels during those years include the Pacific Islands and Europe.

In 1977, we went to the Bahamas. While there we caught dozens of mahi-mahis (dolphin fish). On the way home, we stopped over in New York and saw the King and I on Broadway starring Yul Brenner. "Super entertainment!" I wrote in my journal.

That same year, I went scuba diving in Yaquina and had my first open water dive. It was cold and very strenuous, but a great adventure, so I looked forward to more diving.

In October of that year, we explored Fiji and then went to New Zealand and Australia where we visited with business associates. What a difference from my previous business travels! I wrote in my journal, "It's really so much nicer to have little Fernie with me. There's a lot less pressure also since I sold the business and can take a slower pace."

In 1978, we went to Greece with my brother Bob, Gail, and Bill and Sue Short. Departing on May 18, we celebrated my birthday pretty much every day of the trip. On the third day, we boarded a Viking sailboat. We ended the travels on the beach in Santorini, where there were "a few nudies...Bill and Bob are having trouble with where to look," I wrote in my journal.

In July 1979 when our three-year contract expired, a representative from Multifoods took Myles and I out for a farewell dinner, officially ending my Smoke-Craft days. It was the end of quite an era, and I was ready for the next one.

Fern visiting with her sister Dorothy, late 1970s

In Black Butte with the family, Jennifer, Fern, Mike, Gail, Bobbie, and Chris, 1980

Chapter Eight

Semi-Retirement
1979 to 2006

WITH THE KIDS ALL OFF LIVING THEIR LIVES, the house was quiet in Albany, except when we had friends over for dinner. I skied a lot in winter and played a lot of tennis year-round. We traveled to visit our kids. We spent time with family locally. My parents and brother still lived in Albany. And our neighborhood was never boring, like the day my neighbor and friend Bill Scharpf got rich quick with Nike.

A Nike Surprise

In our immediate neighborhood, there were about fifteen houses, and, of course, we all knew each other quite intimately. Bill lived across the street and down on the corner. He had a personal history with the Nike company, which started in Eugene, Oregon, as Blue Ribbon Sports in 1964. The track coach at University of Oregon, Bill Bowerman, along with a runner named Phil Knight, started Nike to design better running shoes for their team, and Bill's brother, George Scharpf ran on the track team with Coach Bowerman. Consequently, George worked for the company in its earliest years, fundraising to help get it going. I helped him a little by spreading the word and invested a bit, owning a few shares. George unfortunately passed away fairly young. He left his stock to his brother Bill, totaling about 6,000 shares.

Some ten years later in December 1980 on a cold morning, I looked out my front window to see Bill running out into the intersection, waving his arms and jumping up and down, yelling, "I'm rich! I'm rich!"

I went outside and called, "What are you screaming about, Bill?"

"Nike went public!" He said. The papers had just announced it. The price per share skyrocketed. Bill became a multimillionaire overnight. He didn't need the money. He owned a lumberyard. But we could always get thrilled about money. I could still see that scene vividly while writing this book some 38 years later.

Burning Leaves

A silly story that stands out illustrates the understanding and comradery of our neighborhood in Albany, and I guess a little something about me. It was the 1980s in autumn, leaves everywhere. I raked them up into the ditch beside the road and threw a match in and started burning them. Why wouldn't you do that?

As the smoke rose, Bill Scharpf along with my neighbor Russ Tripp came jogging towards me from the intersection. Russ said smoke was drifting into his house and asked me if I wouldn't mind putting out the fire. The leaves were burning pretty good by then, so I apologized and assured him that after it calmed down, I'd speed it along and move the location. We all stood on my front lawn. Bill said, "And be careful. That's against the law to burn those leaves in the ditch. The police will get you."

I said, "I don't worry about the police. I can take care of them."

"Well," said Russ, "Maybe. But the police chief is standing right there." The chief, who also lived in our neighborhood had walked over and was standing behind us on the lawn.

I had to let the fire burn quite a bit before I could put it out. It was too hot. I was embarrassed, but they were all very good-natured about it.

Self-Stor Moves to Florida, 1980s

All during this time, I did continue working with my various enterprises and investments, which I enjoyed, but only part-time. After the fall-out with Rocky, I still had the storage units with others managing them, and they were still a wonderful money-maker.

Around the time I fully retired, my son Mike received an advanced real estate degree which included securities and commercial investment. Taking these classes provided a platform of knowledge and motivation for him, and so he approached me to do some business together. I was excited to partner with my son.

We started by purchasing a small apartment complex in McMinnville called the Adams Street Apartments (19 units). The next purchase was a storage facility in Vancouver Washington called KODA Storage Center. I was a partial investor when he started a Mortgage Company called Crown Mortgage in Portland. The venture never got too far off the ground, but he learned a lot.

In 1984, Mike learned from a family friend that Orlando, Florida, was a great place for real estate and investment properties. In January of 1986 he accepted a position as an investment specialist with Coldwell Banker (now CBRE) in Orlando, and he and his family moved there. A couple years later, he approached me to see if I would consider investing in a self-storage opportunity in Orlando. The structure would be: he would find the land, obtain all the permits, arrange financing, hire the General Contractor, oversee construction, and start a management company to lease it up. I would help finance it and add my two cents. Sounded good to me!

Bobbie, Jennifer, Fern, Mike, Gail, me and Chris, 1985

Our first deal was called Lakehurst, and shortly thereafter we did another one called Kirkman Road. The third one was Central Parkway in Altamonte Springs.

The first storage deal was a complicated structure involving a 1031 exchange for the Woodvillage Parcel in Oregon. We later arranged 1031 exchanges out of all the Oregon storage properties into storage properties in Florida with the entire family investing. The primary family deals were known as Kissimmee, Apopka, and Lakehurst. Mike arranged a couple more storage deals that involved just Fern and me. We helped Mike with his first couple of bank loans, which had become much more complicated since I was his age, but just those first ones. Then he was off and running on his own.

All of these properties grew to be very successful in their operations and value. In 1994, he signed a joint venture agreement to partner with Shurgard Storage Centers to assist them in growing their Florida portfolio. While he built, purchased, managed, and oversaw some 40 storage centers in Florida between 1994 and

2005, Fern and I and some of his sisters were passive investors. The Florida Storage properties continued to be successful for many years. We sold out of Florida in 2016 and out of that business for me entirely.

The Savings and Loan Goes to the Suits

State Savings and Loan was very successful until literally "the suits" walked in. In 1983 these federal agents in pinstripe suits with chips on their shoulders arrived at our door. Representing the federal government, they said, "You're bankrupt" and closed us. We weren't bankrupt, but there had been some dishonest S&L's, and they started closing them all.

We had to give the money back to the stockholders. Fortunately, we were able to divest our stock and with the real estate we owned and good business practices, there was a surplus, and so we made money. No one who banked with us or invested in us lost out.

This was several years before the big S&L scandal. When the Feds took over our bank, they renamed it State Federal Savings and Loan and moved the headquarters to Corvallis. It had its first ever loss that year and collapsed in 1985. In 1988, my partner Whit and I were accused of negligence and fraud by the FSLIC in connection with the collapse, which was ridiculous. It was a dirty, unfair suit. We offered to settle, but they wanted even more money. It was unsettling. In the meantime, Fern and I had plans to go to Hawaii, so I tried to put it aside for a while.

I described that trip to Hawaii in 1988 in one of my journals as "probably the best ever." We stayed in Hana, experienced marvelous beach time, fun snorkeling, lots of tennis and golf, good weather, and a nice time with Rich and Sharon Hews.

While there, I received a welcome call from my attorney John Arnold, telling us it was going to be a $25,000 settlement (plus $15,000 to Arnold) for the S&L business. Good news at last! But still, it left me with mixed feelings, both relief and infuriation.

Soon after, I went to Portland to sign off on the settlement. It was a giant case of blackmail, and they claimed it was justified and legal. I wrote in my journal at the time, "Why is it legal to sue an innocent person on trumped up charges and be insulated from countersuit?"

The bank was reorganized as Freedom Federal, purchased by Washington Federal Savings & Loan with the assistance of the FSLIC. By 1989, there were criminal trials of four other people accused of fraud and conspiracy in the collapse of 1985. The whole thing was a mess!

Finally Taking Up Golf

I finally took up golf in earnest in the 1980s. One of my best friends growing up, Bud Fortier, was definitely an influence in me taking up golf. He and some of my buddies played on the high school golf team, but working at the butcher shop after school and playing baseball and a little football and writing for the newspapers, I didn't have time to play eighteen or even nine holes back then.

While building and managing Smoke-Craft, the 70-hour-plus work weeks and business travel certainly didn't allow me time for golf, even though I belonged to the golf course and country club Bud and his dad built. I felt about golf the same way I felt about playing card games. "I don't have time to sit down for that!" I told my kids, "I can do that when I'm 80!"

I was approaching 60 years when I was ready to take up the sport. Ahead of schedule! But I pondered, "How am I going to learn the game?"

I decided to watch professional golfers on television and imitate them. I'd turn on a golf tournament on TV, watch one of the pro's swing, taking in all the details of it, standing and trying it a few times without a club while watching. Then, I'd go out on the patio with a club. It had sliding glass doors that reflected my image. I swung the club again and again, watching myself until my swing resembled the one I saw the pro use. Then I practiced it on the driving range and pitching and putting greens. People used to tell me, "You have a perfect swing," which was nice. I was just imitating what I saw. And I worked at it. I complemented this with a couple lessons here and there.

From then on, I enjoyed golf, playing in Albany, Palm Desert and around the world during our travels, although for many years I still never played golf as much as I did tennis. Tennis continued to be my primary sport in the sunshine, and I enjoyed almost daily tennis matches with frequent tournaments.

Winning a Senior Tournament

The pinnacle moment in my golfing "career" was the Northwest Seniors Championship, the annual tournament put on by the Northwest Seniors Golf Association. The Association was made up of senior persons (55+) living in the states of Idaho, Oregon, and Washington. There were some four hundred members, including me.

Once I had my swing down and had been playing a little while, I decided, why not, I'd try competing in the Northwest Seniors Championship. It was my first ever golf tournament.

I drove up to the Portland Golf Course, which was new at the time, about 75 miles from Albany, every day for two weeks to play in the tournament. Two hundred men competed in match play.

The trophy from the Seniors tournament

Well, I won my first match. Then I won the next. And then the next, until miraculously, I made it into the final game. I was two down from the leader going into the second nine. My opponent, an experienced player, had won the tournament the previous two years, and yet I managed to match him on every hole. Then towards the end of our final nine, he hit a ball out of bounds, giving me a chance to catch up.

I ended up beating him by two strokes. It was surprising and exciting. I was presented with a gorgeous, big trophy the size of a kitchen table. Of course, they kept that one and added my name to it, giving me a smaller one to take home. My picture even appeared in the sporting section of the Portland paper, but I didn't need anybody to make a fuss about it. Just winning it was very satisfying for me.

Lost Ball

I had one hole-in-one during my golfing days in 1990. It was a par 3, 182 yards uphill from the tee box at Black Butte. I was playing with my brother. I teed off, and the ball flew high in the air over the hill towards the green, but when we got there, I couldn't find it. We looked and looked and looked for my golf ball. Bob finally said, "Well, did you look in the hole?" There it was. He screamed and hollered. We figured that I actually overshot the hole by some 50 feet, but lucky for me, it rolled back downhill, onto the green and right into the hole. That was pretty exhilarating.

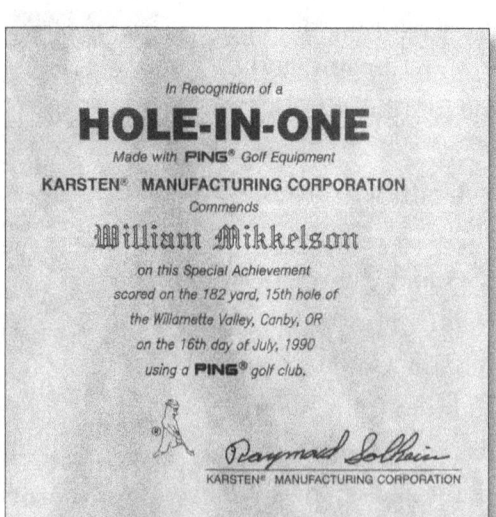

A Place in Palm Desert

In the early 1980s, Fern and I rented a home in Rancho Las Palmas in Rancho Mirage and liked it so much, we bought a home. We started going there regularly for weeks or months at a time during the winter. The sunshine was wonderful. We played lots of tennis, golf, made new friends, and hosted long-time friends and family.

It's been pretty nice living part-time in paradise! Palm Desert, circa 2000

It also provided me with more opportunities to fly. I kept my airplane at the Palm Springs airport. Sometimes I'd just get in it to fly around for fun. Sometimes we used it to get somewhere. In 1983, for example, I flew to Mazatlan via Palm Springs. I used it to go on multiple fishing trips. And Fern and I used it to get back and forth from Albany and the desert and to visit the kids and grandkids. I made several trips to the Oshkosh airshow from Albany and liked to bring items back such as the year I brought back three large boxes of fireworks which were illegal in Oregon. I flew any chance I could get!

In the 1990s, a lot of our desert friends moved to a new development in Palm Desert called The Lakes, so we followed them. In 1997, we purchased a home on Lookout Drive in the development. Friends from Albany joined us for a house-warming party, 36 in attendance. We stayed there off and on from mid-February to the beginning of May every year from then on, except when we were traveling.

As a result, we met and made even more new friends and renewed old friendships as well. The events of that year, as I recalled them in my journal, provides a good example of our time in the desert. To paraphrase:

I improved my golf and tennis game by playing so much. The kids and grandkids came for visits throughout the season. We enjoyed a big tennis club party. I won a 3.5 tennis singles tournament. I flew my plane a lot, once to Borrego for lunch and back, another time to Nevada with the Riesens. The ladies gambled, and Al Riesen and I played golf at a course renowned as the hardest in Nevada. It was great fun. For the last five weeks, I was pleased to find and join a new bible study group. It was a great winter in the desert sunshine, typical of many great years that followed.

In the 2000s, we moved to a different condo on Wild Horse Drive in The Lakes, also a beautiful place. In later years as golf and tennis faded away, I added water aerobics and personal training to my activities.

Fishing Adventures & a Plane Full of Salmon

Every once in a while, I went on a fishing trip in different locations throughout the 80s, 90s and 2000s, sometimes with Fern, sometimes with friends. In 1984, Fern and I fished on the South Island of New Zealand and visited Auckland and Fiji.

Most often though, I fished in Alaska.

In 1985, Fern and I fished in Alaska with Howard and Janet Harpole. On the way back, we flew into British Columbia, Canada, and ended up at a hotel at Riverview, where a burglar snuck into the Harpole's room during the night and stole all their cash. It was disturbing. Lucky for Fern and me, our door was too squeaky for someone to open it!

Fern and Janet Harpole as we get ready to fly to Alaska, 1985

One time I flew a couple guys up to Alaska to go fishing during a salmon run. We had to fly over the Canadian border to get there, and one guy had a pistol with him. Any time you fly into Canadian air space and plan to land, you have to stop for inspection at the border. I told him if you're caught with a pistol when we're inspected, they'll put you in prison, so I assumed he got rid of it. We crossed the border and I asked him, "What did you do with that pistol?"

"Oh, it's right here," he replied. I turned the plane around. We had to fly back another ten minutes, back into the U.S. to get rid of his gun.

Once we made it to Canada, I landed in a field on a small airstrip. I had made prior arrangements for a helicopter to pick us up there and take us to this waterfall in Katmai National Park where the salmon were running. It was amazing! There were thousands of salmon jumping up the falls into the rushing water.

We spent two or three days there, catching all the salmon we could possibly imagine. I fileted them all out, being the butcher.

Places Visited in "Retirement"

This is a partial list of our travels, fun to reflect on when you put it all together!

- Spain
- Portugal
- Africa
- Mexico
- Alaska
- Egypt
- Turkey
- Europe: France, Paris, etc.
- Switzerland for skiing
- Russia
- China
- South America: Argentina, etc.
- San Juan Islands
- Hawaii
- Ireland
- Israel (with Southwest Community Church)
- Greece
- Italy
- Australia many
- New Zealand
- Cruises (including the islands of British Columbia), and personal flights, long and short

There was no use taking all the heads and tails home. At the end, I had a big case of beautiful salmon for us to carry home, about 100 pounds worth.

Returning to my Cessna, we took off to return to Albany. I started circling and circling, aiming for a hole in the clouds. I got up to nearly 15,000 feet, and I just couldn't get us any higher. There was just too much weight in the little plane.

I returned to the air strip, and we assessed the situation. We had 100 pounds of salmon. Each of the guys weighed 200 pounds. We had to offload some baggage.

Now, these guys were somewhat indebted to me. I paid the gas and flew them up there. I saved one of them from a possible prison sentence or fine for having a weapon. And we didn't want to lose our salmon.

So, what do you think I left behind? The two guys!

I took the salmon and went home. The two fellows had to take a bus and find their way home. It was the only way to get the salmon home before it spoiled. The flight was about 90 minutes to the border to land and clear and another hour to Albany. It took them much longer to get home. But we laughed about it afterwards, enjoying our salmon dinners.

Along with the Salmon run, I had other fishing and fowl hunting adventures, like pheasant hunting with friends in 1986.

Time with Kids and Grandkids

We spent a lot of time visiting the kids and grandkids during the 1980s. All of them had families of their own by then. Time never stands still! We visited Gail, Paul and kids in Sebastopol. Walking with little Alicia, she turned to me and said, "It sure is fun to walk with you, Grandpa." What a nice reward!

Flying High

What a joy becoming grandparents!
Fern and I holding Doug and Aaron Miller, 1979

Mike and Melissa and their kids lived in Florida. We were doing business together, but always made time to play, one time staying on St. Augustine beach in a big condo, watching the grandkids learn to surf. It was great that Bobbie and John and the girls lived close in Salem. We visited with them and sometimes the other kids at the Black Butte house too. We saw Jennifer and Justin and their kids in Portland, and of course visited them when they moved to Vancouver, Washington, in 1989. Each time we saw the kids, whether it was with the arrival of a new grandchild or just to spend time with everyone, we arrived back home satisfied every time after the reacquaintance with our family.

Backpacking, 1983

Hawaii, 1984

World Travel

When I officially retired from Smoke-Craft/Multi-Food in 1979, Fern was ready for more travel. Just for fun. I was too. So, we did. My primary work over time became fun.

We had many memorable trips. Fern and I would discuss where we wanted to go and make plans. Of course, I wanted to go to Denmark since Danish is a large part of my heritage. There are seventeen columns of Mikkelsons in the Copenhagen phonebook, spelled exactly like that too. Only it's pronounced "Mickelson" there. One time, we stayed on a working ranch in Montana, riding horses and relaxing and visiting the ghost town of Castle City and Glacier National Park.

We traveled to Israel, touring biblical sites with a group from our church in the desert, the Southwest Community Church of Indian Wells. In 1988, I skied in Switzerland, a thrilling experience. Among our many cruises, we sailed through the islands of British Columbia.

For just about every trip we took, I kept a daily travel journal. This had been my habit for a long time. I started my first daily diary in 1935 and was influenced by my time writing for the school and our local newspaper when I was in high school. Fern often kept them too.

Here are a few highlights from our travel journals. I sure was blessed to experience these things!

Thailand, 1980

In November 1980 we had a wonderful adventure in Thailand where we toured Bangkok and Penang and other cities. In Penang, I wrote in my journal, "Fern and I each had a massage, which felt absolutely terrif, then a super foam bath. Mm. A little disco then nighty." Our hotel balcony overlooked the beach. "Multi-colored sails, white sand and ocean palms make a romantic setting." Singapore was also amazing.

 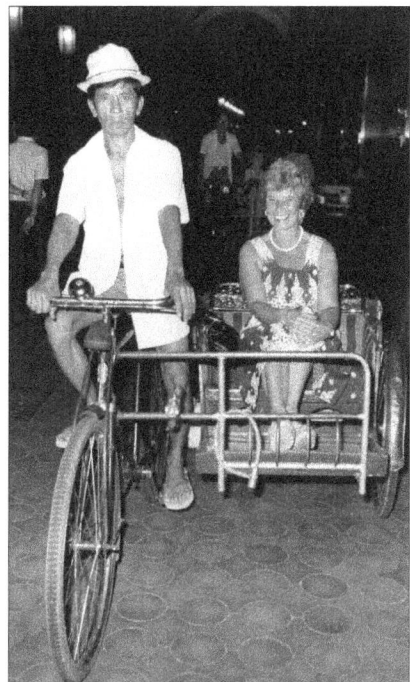

Singapore, 1980

Our 42nd Anniversary in China & Hong Kong, 1987

In 1987, we went to China as part of a business exchange, landing in Beijing. We toured Tiananmen Square and the Forbidden City. We walked the Great Wall. For one meeting with the Chinese businessmen, our leader George Chandler asked if I would be chairman. It was a nice recognition and good opportunity but exhausting, requiring most of my mental and physical resources to perform well and keep the meeting under control while pausing for an interpreter with every exchange. As we progressed, the Chinese became more interested and started to participate. Then it was our turn to learn from them. It was a stimulating experience.

After China, we went on to Hong Kong, where Fern and I celebrated our forty-second anniversary. What a beautiful setting and emotional remembrance in a dining room overlooking Victoria Harbor among people who had become our special friends during our three weeks of travel together. Fernie gave me a present of "Iron Balls." Could that have been symbolic?

Stopping in Korea, we headed home from there.

Circa 1979 (my perm days)

Spain & Portugal, 1990

In September 1990, Fern and I took a five-week trip to Spain and Portugal with Brother Bob and Gail. As much as I loved these travel adventures, I also loved my daily life at home. I had mixed emotions, leaving Oregon during its most beautiful season, not seeing close ones for five weeks, away from business and news channels. But in the end, I concluded, "Oh well! Guess we'll just push off and immerse ourselves in pleasure!"

We flew to Spain sitting in "dream seats" aboard a new 767, the first seats in first class. Wow! Soon after we landed, we found ourselves in a small Fiat crammed full of our bags, and the adventures on land began. We toured all over the country, taking in sights that included the Prado art museum in Barcelona, cathedrals, beaches and views along the Atlantic coastline. We enjoyed good meals and nice accommodations. We spent one evening at the Hotel Parador atop a hill drinking sangria and overlooking Toledo. An absolutely inspiring view! We took a guided tour of Gibraltar, a chance of a lifetime.

One evening at Quinta Patricia above Lisbon, Portugal, we all sat out on the veranda a hundred feet above the city almost totally enchanted with the view as the city lights began to glimmer like hundreds of fallen stars. We were awe struck to see the moon, as though preplanned, rise over the horizon, a dark orange orb that brightened to a beautiful cheese color as it climbed in the sky and bathed the entire hillside. This experience was one of a life time and never to be forgotten!

And I still found opportunities to work out, swim, golf, and play tennis all throughout the trip, essential not just for fun but my well-being.

Africa, 1991

I spent my 67th birthday in "Wild Africa," Kenya, with Fern and Chris and Tom, who were part of the tour group. We were surrounded by animals, gazelles leaping and running, showing off their speed, baboons fighting, and an elephant spraying himself with his trunk and wading into the Ewaso Ngiro River, a river as wide as the Willamette. It all reminded me vividly of where we were, in Africa. Wow!

That afternoon we saw a male lion across the river and then driving further, found two mamas and five cubs lying in the sand on the river bank. What a thrill as we approached and saw the family scene unfold. The "old lady" stood poised, alert on a higher bank overlooking the others as they frolicked and napped on the beach, probably having just feasted on a gazelle or gerenuk.

Heading "home" to the Samburu Lodge, hot, dirty and tired, I ripped off my clothes and had a cool beer on the porch overlooking the river as night crept in. So very relaxing!

Leaving for dinner we saw genet cats roaming wild outside. The chef made me a cake that read "Happy Birthday Bill." Completely unexpected and such a thrill to me that I teared up. We created great memories during those two wonderful days and nights at Samburu National Reserve.

Our next stop was the Mount Kenya Safari Club. On the way we stopped to take pictures of camels, and some locals came running and shouting and waving sticks at us, threatening harm unless we paid. We soon learned that just months before, six cars were robbed and two persons killed at that spot, so we were happy to reach our destination!

Mount Kenya Safari Club was a great place, very luxurious. After golf with Tom at the adjacent country club, we had dinner, returning to our rooms to find a fire in the fireplace, hot water bottles under the bedcovers, and chocolates on our pillows.

Chris and Tom returned home, and Fern and I went on from there flying over Aberdares Mountains and across the Rift Valley, landing at Masai Mara National Reserve, contiguous with the Serengeti National Park in Tanzania.

We went by Land Rover to our tent camp, our own 12x20-foot two-bed room with a lovely large adjoining tile bathroom. Lunch was nice, almost like eating at Bryant's Park back home. It seemed incongruous to be waited on so well when we were staying in a tent—albeit a nice one—in the African grassland.

The game experience in Masai Mara was totally different than Samburu, because the landscape in the Serengeti was mostly rolling grass plains spotted with umbrella-like acacia trees. Out on the savannah, we saw lions napping, a leopard, more gazelles, impalas and a topi, lots of wart hogs, and more. We returned at the end of the day "bumped out" from the four-wheeling and tired.

During dinner that evening, our personal waiter suddenly arrived at our table and said, "Hippo mister wanna see?" A big hippo was just on the other side of the canvas!

As we were bedding down we heard whoompa, whoompa and lots of grunting, a bevy of wild screeches, barking and grunting noises. It was Africa alright!

We went on to take a 12-passenger balloon ride over an elephant herd. We saw more game in the safari the next day, including giraffes and zebras. We toured the Karen Blixen estate (the real Out of Africa setting). We swam in the warm Indian Ocean off Serena Beach in Mombasa and took a boat to the reefs. We took in beautiful Victoria Falls near Bulawayo, Zimbabwe, the roar of the water unending, the sight of those wide, powerful falls almost magnetic. A precious reward for the long trip, probably 12,000 miles! We took in a gold reef tour, which turned out to be very interesting. We took the exciting and luxurious blue train to Capetown, South Africa, and enjoyed wine-tasting in the South African wine country. There were even more memorable moments before we flew to Orlando and back to home. It was amazing!

One other time we traveled to Africa and went on a safari, this time with brother Bob and Gail. We rode giraffes and elephants and did everything that tourists do there. I got a kick out of my brother. He's really businesslike. He was riding a giraffe, the ride costing about fifteen dollars. When the ride was finished, the guide said, "That will be five dollars to get off," and you know what my brother said? "I'm not getting off." So, who won? My brother. He just didn't budge from that hump until they finally said, "Okay, get off."

That's kind of the way he was. If he went into a restaurant and had his daughter or my girls with him, and the waiter said, "What will you guys have?" He'd challenge that. He'd say, "Do you see all guys here?" I got a kick out of that.

Flying Turbo

Over the years, I ended up owning a number of different airplanes, varieties of the Piper Cub, the Cirrus, a couple Cessnas, but in November 1993, I had my eye on something more powerful than I'd ever flown before.

Chris and the Cirrus

Flying my Cessna Centurion 210

Semi-Retirement

My friend Rob McCracken flew my buddy Jack Kasper and me to Portland in my Cessna 210 to catch a commercial flight to Boulder, Colorado, for the grand showing of our new plane: a Cheyenne Piper turbo dual-prop! After a nine-month search for just the right one, actually walking into the hangar and seeing it was a thrilling climax, the slow warming Quartz lights in the building getting brighter and brighter and gradually filling my eyes with the most gorgeous, glimmering beauty in all my plane life! The culmination of a dream perhaps, a $350,000 turboprop, a gigantic jump from a piston single to a turbine twin.

That was a busy Saturday. I had been nominated for the Distinguished Citizen Award by the Albany Chamber of Commerce and had to write a letter to excuse myself from the festivities that were taking place that evening. The plane was worth it.

After spending the night in Boulder, Jack checked me out for the flight home in the Cheyenne Piper. What a smooth and powerful beast! It was even fun to taxi. We landed at Twin Falls for lunch before continuing on to Salem, with about four hours logged. I flew the plane to Redmond and landed! That same day, I flew to Cameron Park, circled and flew back again to get used to all the new gadgets. What fun!

In the afternoon, I flew to Palm Springs to meet Fern, who had driven down while I was heli-skiing just prior to the trip to Boulder. It took only two hours in the air, the DME at one point indicating 310 knots! I landed the new jet for the second time. It was great to see Fern. I guess I felt like I owned the whole world. At least I had the best part!!

It was too bad we were leaving for Mazatlán, Mexico, the next day. Of course, that was fun too, but I couldn't wait to fly the Piper again.

When I did, practicing landings and take-offs, it was exhilarating to learn and be challenged. Again, I reflected what a big jump it was from a reciprocating turbo 210 with 300 HP to the twin 650 shaft HP with Pratt and Whitney jet engines. I wondered if I had made the right decision, but I couldn't hesitate or put it off at age 69. $350,000 was a bunch of money! It helped once the Cessna 210 was sold that I owed $150k instead of the entire amount.

The entire time I owned it, I continued to assess if the plane was right for me with all its power. But it was fun.

In winter of 1993, I took advantage of the plane's speed and flew the Cheyenne II turbo jet plane alone 210 miles just to have a nice dinner with Jenny and the family up in Washington. Afterwards, I said so-long and flew home with the full moon keeping me company, reminding me how much I love to fly!

With the Chyenne II turbo, 1993

There's Nothing Like a Mikkelson Christmas!

Just like in my childhood, Christmas was always special in adulthood, especially when the kids joined us for the holidays.

From one of my journals:

Sunday Christmas 1988

Gail, Paul and wunderkids are here!

Such a joy to wake up and have little child noises coming from the upstairs bedrooms once again! They truly are loving, beautiful kids and are being taught to be considerate and polite—much more a delight and fun to play with.

I went to church alone while Fern cooked and worked on finishing wrapping, charging batteries, and all the other preparations.

All families started arriving about 2:00 p.m. Paul and Gail were already there, Rob, Chris and their three boys, John and Bobbie with Emily and Anne, Jennifer and Justin with Grant and Jenna. Brother Bob and wife Gail brought my mother. About 20 of us always filled the dining room for the holiday meal, and we added kid's tables, too.

We opened presents creating pandemonium. Paper flew everywhere. Wow!

Then we had a nice peaceful pork loin-turkey dinner.

It was so nice to have everyone here and to have the time to visit. Mike and Melissa phoned from Florida and talked to all of us. Their family of four were with us in spirit, as it seemed that's as close as we were going to get to having all five of our kids together this year. But they would be visiting us the next week.

I sure could tell the kids were maturing because they were well behaved and quieter, even when Paul stirred them up!

Another blessed, super, wonderful Christmas.

Santa Bob

The memorable moment of Christmas 1989 was when Santa arrived at about 5 p.m. and surprised everyone by stomping on the roof and peeking in the skylight. It was brother Bob in the red suit!

In the early years, a traditional Christmas was Christmas Eve at my Mom and Dad's (Alice and Harry) with Mom's famous Christmas cookies and clam chowder. After church on Christmas Day, Fern's parents and others would join us at our home for Christmas dinner.

Any time was a good time with the family! 1990s

Physical Challenges from Age

With age comes physical challenges, back and neck issues in 1988, a torn hernia and prostate infection in 1989. The last two required surgery. I went in on a Thursday, Fern taking good loving care of me, and on Saturday I was playing golf. In 1990, I had skin treatment and surgery on the inside of my cheeks with anesthesia to put me out. That was on a Monday. I walked for a little exercise and nursed it for a couple days, proud of myself for not getting restless and Thursday, I played tennis. The doctor took the stitches out later that day. It was always hard for me if I couldn't be active, like after my water-skiing stunt and a couple intense heli-skiing experiences I'll soon reveal. But Fern and I were fortunate to have good health most of our lives.

Retirement was an adjustment, but I got used to it! By 1990, I reflected in my journal: "I'm enjoying many days of pleasure and great changes in lifestyle since the only requirements are to eat, sleep and enjoy! Is this the true retirement we and everyone always yearns for?" How lucky I was!

Some Investments Just Don't Pan Out

Along with sports, I stayed active in investing when I saw a promising venture. In the 1990s, I invested in entrepreneurs from Oregon State University, who developed a water filtration system called Hydro-tech. It could take dirty, contaminated water and filter it to become drinkable. It should have been highly successful, but production was halted due to a fire just as the business was opening. Lawsuits followed, and it fell through. Like the flying car, it lost me some of my personal investment. You win some; you lose some.

An Achievement and Award

In June 1993, I experienced a big achievement. The YMCA Heritage Foundation was finally established! It was an program we had wanted to establish for a while. Through the foundation, individuals could make lasting gifts through their estates to support the principles of the YMCA and to serve more children and families.

We started with about $13,000 with the goal of $100,000 for the year, and it looked like we had good prospects that included a new stock offering of Metro One.

In 1994 came the awards banquet for those people receiving the Distinguished Service Award from the Albany Area Chamber of Commerce. I was home to attend it. It was quite a humbling experience.

Fern and I dressed up for the evening. What a gala affair, with 260 people present, a capacity audience! The hall was nicely decorated and a swing band played. All four of my daughters were there, causing Fern and I to swell with pride. So many friends were there too. As the ceremonies began, many rose to speak. To have them preach such salutatory stuff about me was quite embarrassing. But at the same time, it was such an incredible feeling. I had to keep from getting confused. Was this really the person I was hearing about when they read the "accomplishments?"

There were so many other well-deserving nominees. The short speech from me at the microphone was difficult, and I'll never remember what I said but will always recollect the sensation of warmth as my friends and family looked up at me, smiling and applauding. I had to hold back the tears of emotion as I tried to condense all the memories of 40 years into one short evening.

Sailing the British Virgin Isles, October 1995

Our travel adventures continued with sailing and diving around the Virgin Isles. We spent a lot of time sitting on the back deck of our ship with the sun rising, a gentle breeze and warm, humid air. Fernie was dripping sweat most of the time (and had a horrible cold), but found ways to enjoy the new experience anyway.

We took a break from the water to motor across Peter Island, where I snorkeled. The water was wonderful, warm, green and refreshing. The whole scene reminded me of Lake Shasta in California, only greatly expanded.

We dove on a shipwreck, which was exciting. With painful ear trouble, I had to go slow, taking about 10 minutes to reach bottom at approximately 85 feet below. The wreck was a steel vessel lost in the worst hurricane ever in 1867. It had been the first prop-driven steam vessel of its age, 300 feet long. The sight was unbelievable, and it was a comfy dive once I got oriented.

We went on to cruise to Virgin Gorda. The sailing was great, and I got to "steer," entered into the record log at 10.1 knots! That was fun but got to be less so after an hour. We motored around and toured all three of the Virgin Islands on the tour. I dove and snorkeled frequently, swimming with sting rays and jelly fish. It was a wonderful adventure.

New York, October 1996

During our trip to the Big Apple in 1996, we toured the World Trade Towers and Radio City Theatre. We rode the subway and were thrilled by fast cabs. We also did a lot of walking. While there, we saw four Broadway plays. Sunset Boulevard was very well done. Cats was no good at all. A Funny Thing Happened on the Way to the Forum was great. Les Miserables was superior! I have never experienced singing and music so wonderful!

We went on from there to enjoy fall foliage and historical sites in Connecticut and Massachusetts. It felt comfy to get home and also satisfying to look back and cherish the times we just had.

Kayaking Trip in the San Juan Islands, 1997

On our trip to the San Juan Islands, I decided to go kayaking. It was my first time in a kayak. Lots of people kayak there as a way to tour the islands and see wildlife like the orcas and bald eagles that frequent the area. Fern didn't want to go, so I went solo. The lady at the rental company put me in a kayak with a paddle and said, "Now, go that way, take two lefts and then a right. Then you're under a waterfall. So, watch out for the waterfall." Away I went by myself.

I had been paddling about two-hours when I took a break and went to shore. When I put my hand on a rock to pull myself in, a little robin hopped up to me and pecked my hand as if it was saying, "Hi, how are you doing?" Then it flew away. When I made it to the waterfall, I felt great relief that I hadn't gotten lost. Then I made my way back. It was an exciting undertaking.

Christmas Trip to Huatulco, Mexico, 1997

As Fern and I rode in the Miller's Suburban to the airport, it was a jolly atmosphere, but seemed strange to be going away for Christmas.

Once we arrived at Club Med in Huatulco, Mexico, however, it was a grand reunion, and seven days of family fun began.

Each day, we ate from massive buffets with an unbelievable variety of food. The activities were many. Eric liked archery, all the Millers enjoyed basketball. Becca and Alicia were into acting. Becca, Eric and William all performed in the evening shows. William was into sharks. And all the kids were busy all day long.

Mexico, 1997

There was even a circus area with a high trapeze, quite a novelty. The Millers kayaked, surfed, sailed and more. Tennis was fun for me, but hot and sweaty.

On Christmas Eve, Club Med put on a very extravagant dinner party that used the entire soccer field, with fancy lighting, wild music and gourmet food. Before dinner was a performance of dancers representing five different countries in costumes.

Paul arranged a boat trip with locals, and nine of us went. We saw an eagle eating a fish it had just caught, the view of several farms along the shore, and interesting rock formations. We snorkeled into a cave in the rocks, a colorful, eerie and dramatic experience. On the way back, Eric caught a three-foot barracuda. Talk about excited!

The only snafu was our missing luggage, which didn't arrive for three days. We borrowed razors, pills, cosmetics and the like.

On Christmas Day, we had the most wonderful Mikkelson Family morning worship service, all 21 members of our party present on a small private beach, a gorgeous setting as small waves broke on the rocks and sand. It was only us and God! Each person had his Mikkelson Fiesta Familia t-shirt on and we sang, prayed, read the Christmas Story from the Bible and each shared goals or expectations for his or her new year. It was absolutely the nicest, most precious moment God could provide for our family.

After wrapping and sorting presents we had brought, we took them all to a small nearby town and gave them to the local kids. None of us had ever experienced anything like this. What a great feeling sharing those gifts. It was warming to watch our kids as they prepared and shared.

We went to Mexico again in 2001 when I was 76 years old with all the family who could make it, this time to Ixtapa/Zihuatanejo, Mexico. Christmas once again great. We all contributed to a new church building there as our gift to the community. A wonderful feeling!

The Mikkelson Family in Mexico, 2001

Lake Shasta Better with Family and Friends

In July 1997, we drove down to Lake Shasta to go houseboating and waterskiing, as usual. But that particular time, Mike had rented a new wide tip Connelly ski, and at 7:15 before breakfast, I tried "the Big One," as we called it. What a great way to start the day! We did lots of reading and sunning on the houseboat. Those days at Shasta meant a lot to me. As I reflected in my journal that July, "I am receiving special benefits from being here with the group of family and near family, new confidence and reawakening some very real inner peace. Perhaps when I return to Fernie and friends, I can contribute more and be closer by being still and listening."

A New Home in Albany

In 1997, Fern and I decided to build a new home in North Albany. We designed it ourselves, working with an architect and asking each other, "What do you want in your dream house?"

Semi-Retirement

Another trip, a cruise through the Caribbean Isles, 1997

We knew we wanted large windows to take in the great views and a big deck on the second level. From our lot, you could see a hundred miles on a clear day, monumental Mount Jefferson in the foreground and Mount Hood near Portland in the distance. As the contractor was doing finishing work, we included details that were important to us, a plate rack here, windows there. And for fun, we had a nine-hole putting green on the back lawn with rocks for obstacles.

In the summer of 1999, Fernie and I moved in after nearly two years of construction! After that long, it surely made me wonder if we should have built it. Was it a waste of time and money? After 38 years in one home (1961 to 1999), it was a big change.

At first it felt strange, learning which switch turned on which light and such, but each day Fernie and I adjusted a little more to living in the new house. Each day it seemed more like home. And it was gorgeous. We had lovely neighbors too, mostly young families who treated us as if we were their grandparents.

Homes in Albany, Oregon

433 West Fourth
637 West Tenth
2242 Calapooia Street
1021 Queen Ave
1075 Queen Ave (next to the combination of grocery store and Harry's Market)
3240 South Liberty Street (beginning in 1961)
1900 NW Cascade Heights Drive (Last home in Albany. Sold in 2010)
Moved to Varenna in Santa Rosa in 2010

Our new home in Cascade Heights

It was hard to get used to being in North Albany though, a bit farther from things after a whole life of living only five minutes from everything. At first, we were five to 10 minutes late for every appointment!

In 2010, however, we looked to the future and thought a retirement community might be a good idea. We found a lovely one called Varenna in Santa Rosa, not too far from where Gail lived, where we could still have our own home, but move into assisted care if and when it was necessary. After 86 years, I no longer lived in Albany, Oregon. Of course, we returned as often as we could to visit friends.

While visiting Albany in 2016, I drove up to Cascade Heights to see how the house looked. The lady who lived there welcomed me in with enthusiasm. I thought she was going to kiss me. She was so happy to meet the person who designed the house. She just loved it and hadn't done much to alter it at all.

Ireland & France, Fall 1999

Just after Labor Day in 1999, Fern and I left for Ireland with the RHM's (brother Bob and Gail) and the Harpoles. The country was very, very green with rolling hills, blue skies and rich farmland. The roads were narrow and the villages quaint, the countryside dotted with clean, little white cottages right out of old, old times. One could imagine the thatched roofs they used to have. As we drove by, an Irish herdsman with a stick gathered sheep out in the fields. The bending green pastures and dark green hedgerows seemed never changing.

At village pubs, we enjoyed the room temperature ale, shepherd's pie, and lamb stew. We stayed at a dairy farm and experienced the warmth of Irish coffee after a typical Irish rain.

Next, we flew to Paris, where we stayed in a gorgeous Chalet. From there, we drove into the countryside, taking in ancient, quaint French towns, and a wine estate chateau. One day we travelled to the end of Burgundy and climbed to a point overlooking the valley. It was very scenic. Below us were several small villages, clusters of homes and shops with steepled churches totally surrounded by fields, no fences, no ad signs. This was typical of what we saw. It was prettier than U.S. land, but the villages had old narrow streets and dark, unpainted buildings, not like most of Ireland, which was colorful. The trip was enlightening and enjoyable.

Italy, 2001

From the Firenze (Florence) airport, we took a bus to Villa Tavalese in Marciella. We had an astounding panoramic view of Elsa Valley from our third-floor room, which had big windows so we almost felt like birds perched on our window sill overlooking the quiet beauty of the valley stretching below. As the day moved into evening, it was even more magnificent taking in God's beauty with the setting sun and changing colors.

We visited among other sights, San Gimignano, known for its many towers, the leaning tower of Pisa, and the cobblestone streets of Lucca. Then we returned to Firenze to take in the city with all its piazzas, statues, and churches. Then came Siena, which dates back to Roman times, 100 B.C. And there was more.

We had mixed feelings when it was time to pack up. We would have liked to have seen and done more, but also "felt" it was time to go home. Another trip that expanded understanding of our world!

We had a lot of fun and advenures over the years!

France, 2006

In 2006, we were back in France, in Marseilles and Arles, but before we left, Fern was experiencing terrible pain in her left arm and neck and ears. We decided to see a French doctor, who came to our room. It was a challenge to communicate. It would have been sort of humorous if it wasn't so serious. The desk lady came and helped interpret between us and the doctor. The doctor diagnosed shingles and gave us a prescription, but the pharmacy was too far away to get there before it closed, and we were flying home the next day. Poor Fernie had to suffer through a 14-hour flight. She was hurting badly.

We finally found ourselves at the Portland airport and made our way to the parking lot and our Buick, but the car wouldn't start due to a dead battery. We got help starting it and finally got home late.

At home, we found some old dental pain pills, and they helped Fern a bit with sleep. After a doctor's appointment the next day and a shower, she could really start healing.

Once Fern was resting comfortably, I went to visit with brother Bob, who was receiving chemo treatments for cancer. These are the trials that can come with age. But we had a good visit.

After a couple days, Bob and Judie came over for lunch. Bob was noticeably weaker and tired easily. Nonetheless, we enjoyed Oxtail soup and had a super time going through a scrapbook he and our sweet Mom had made. The photos, clippings and comments really brought back old times.

Sadly, Bob passed away in December of that year, 2006. For most of our lives, we lived close to each other in Albany. We worked together, played and traveled together, served on several boards and served our community together. Our families remained close all through adulthood. I greatly missed my brother's companionship after he passed away.

With Fern, brother Bob and Gail. I continue to miss my brother.

Give Me a Snow-Covered Mountain!

All during these years, I snow skied regularly at different resorts, occasionally challenging myself with competitions. But when I experienced heliskking—being taken by helicopter to a pristine snowy mountain top to ski long runs in fresh powder—I was hooked! It became my passion, even though a couple times, it could have been the end of me!

Chapter Nine

Ski & Heliskiing Adventures 1975 to 2002

EVERY WINTER I SKIED AS MUCH AS POSSIBLE, as much as work allowed. In my semi-retirement, I was on the slopes frequently. When it came to heliskiing, I wanted to do that as much as I could! How fortunate I was to be able to heli-ski on a regular basis.

The Start of Heliskiing

I first discovered heliskiing in 1975. I had heard about it from friends. One evening, I saw a short advertisement video before the main film in our local movie theater about helicopter ski tours of the mountains in Western Canada, and I realized I knew the folks who started this new company. It looked amazing, so I booked a tour.

After the first time I heli-skied in the Selkirk Mountains in British Columbia, I was hooked! I loved it so much, I saved my money and went every year for some 30 years for a week or two each time.

Top of Revelstoke and ready to ski with CMH (Second from right), 1970s

The company I used most, CMH (Canadian Mountain Heliskiing) grew over the years, acquiring multiple pleasant and well-equipped lodges, some in the valleys and towns at the base of the mountains and some high in the mountains only accessible by helicopter.

Each day, we'd get up, stretch, have breakfast, get our gear together, and get in the helicopter, three to six people in each, and go. The guides looked for the best snow conditions, and the pilots flew us clear up to the ridgelines, parked and let us out on one of the mountains in the finest snow fields that God knows. One day, we'd be on Adamants. Another day on Galena or Revelstoke, Bugaboos, Cariboos, or one of the other peaks in the area. Revelstoke tended to be my favorite. We would ski down following a guide, usually in fresh, undisturbed powder, each run some 20 or 30 minutes long. The helicopter would pick us up at the bottom and take us up again. The goal was always to get in 10 or more runs each day.

Back in the lodge after skiing, we'd soak in a hot tub, maybe get a massage, and have dinner, enjoying the comradery of the group and sharing stories. Some of the guests came year after year like me, and always there were new skiers too. Then we went to bed, and got up to do it again the next day. What fun!

Bill, the Bird (with a Broken Wing!)

Of course, not every heliski run ended perfectly. One time I was leading a group of friends down the mountain and in the canyon ahead of us, I could see a rise that looked fun to jump. Beyond it, I saw there was a tree, but I assessed that there was enough of a clearing to land safely before coming to the tree. And afterwards, the group could gather near the tree to rest before moving on.

Well, I had an expanded opinion of how much landing space the jump required and how fast I was going. I took the rise, flew maybe forty feet, twenty feet in the air, and I landed right in the tree, 12 feet above the ground.

Bugaboos, 1984

Flying High

There I was up in the branches with my skis on and holding my poles, the strangest bird you ever saw.

My first concern was for the people following me. Luckily, they didn't follow my lead jumping over the rise, but instead skied the contours over it and found me up in the tree.

My next concern was the pain in my wrist and back. I could feel that I had twerked my back pretty good.

My friends helped me out of the tree, but my skiing was over for the day.

The next day, I couldn't get up at all. That was okay for the first day. But then on the second day, it got worse, and even worse in the days following. Back at home, I couldn't even get up the stairs to our bedroom. My doctor gave me some pain medicine and told me to lie down most of all day every day for a month, so we had to rent a bed and put it in the living room. Fernie had to babysit me, and I felt bad being in her way. I ended up "living" in the living room for thirty days, sleeping in the rental bed beside the fireplace. I could sit up to read or watch TV, but that was about it. The days were long.

Over time, the pain started to subside, and I followed the doctor's orders until one day, I got up to go to the bathroom and when I came back, the bed was gone.

I asked Fern, "Where's the bed?"

"Well, your thirty days are up," she said.

The rental company had come by and picked up the bed. Going slow, I was able to climb the stairs. It still took a while to get back to my usual level of activity, but it felt good to be out and about again.

Reveling at Revelstoke with Gail, 1990

Heliskiing was most fun for me when I was joined by friends and especially family. Usually it was my son Mike, and one very special time in January 1990 my daughter Gail joined me. It was Gail's first heliskiing experience. I wrote in my journal: "It's hard to realize that Gail is really here with me to help enjoy the delightful pleasure I've known for 15 years up here. 'Generous sacrifice from Paul and I really appreciate it. I only wish all the family and our many friends could take this rare and sensuous exercise."

The powder was sensational, and Gail did really well. It was such a great thrill to watch her and help a bit and see her having fun. We had good hard days of skiing at 17,000 feet in powder and trees, followed by nice meals and time in the hot tub in the evenings.

Ski Jumping Competition, 1990

I liked to challenge myself, so what did I do in my retirement? For two years, I competed in ski jumping. I saw people doing it and thought I'd like to try that. The idea was to go down a fifty-foot or so chute fast, pick up speed, fly off a ramp into the air, and go as far out as you could before landing. It was important to be as streamlined as possible so you could really land a long way down. It was scary but a thrill too. You'd fly seventy or a hundred feet in the air before landing.

Flying High

1970s

    I couldn't even begin to compete with some of the guys who had been jumping since they were six years old. I was starting in my fifties. But I watched and imitated what the experts were doing and tried my best.

    It's a vivid experience, ski jumping. The adrenaline starts pumping even while climbing the stairway up to the top of the slide. There, you look down at the steep white expanse and the awaiting ramp while the helpers up top hold you back. Then you hear them say, "On your mark, get set, go!" They let you go, and you've got to go down. There's nowhere else to go!

    You get low. Gravity takes you. You pick up speed, faster and faster, focused on the approaching chute, the air whipping by. And then you're going off the chute into the air, rising, flying, holding your body and skis in place as you arc down again toward the hill. You have to judge when you're going to land so you can have a nice soft landing. Ninety percent of the rating is the distance that you go and the other ten percent is the form. Down you go at incredible speed, tips in the air to land back of the skis first, bending your knees and then extending your body to absorb the impact.

I'm so grateful for Fern for supporting my ski adventures and joining me on many, even though she would have rather gone to Reno! 1980s

I had the goal of trying ski jumping, and I did it. I didn't excel at it. I didn't beat them all, but I didn't come in last either. Rather quickly, however, I found myself asking, "Why am I doing this?" So, I ended my short competitive ski jumping career. Looking back though, it felt like one of the more courageous things I've done.

Nicknames

It's trying things like ski jumping that landed me the nickname "Wild Bill." I didn't pay much attention to it, but one of my daughters reminded me of it while writing this book. Friends sometimes called me that, especially in regards to my skiing and waterskiing, trying to ski farther and faster, jump farther. I guess I always had nicknames, which in reflection I guess is complimentary. Like my grandfather, guys in high school sometimes called me Mike, short for Mikkelson. My squadron in flight training called me Brushy Bill, because of that toothbrush hanging out of my mouth.

In later years, I carried beef jerky with me to give to friends and family. I became known as The Big Jerk or Mr. Jerky. I got a kick out of that one!

Black Ink Race, 1990

In February 1990, I entered the slalom event in the Black Ink Ski Race at Mount Bachelor. I raced on "Jennifer B's team." In my warm-up run, I almost fell at full speed when I failed to see a hidden knee-high net at the bottom stretched across the finish. It was masked in the shade. I hit it going 30 mph and flew into the air upside down for 25 feet and then hit the snow head down and rolled and slid until I ended 100 feet farther down the hill almost to the flat area wondering what hit me. Wow! It felt like I ripped all the muscles on my left side, but thank God, I was okay.

I got back on my feet and took a couple successful runs on the slalom course that morning. After lunch I took a short nap and did two more runs. I was learning and getting a bit faster. It was fun to compete, but similar to jumping, I didn't need to do it all the time.

Black Ink Race, 1990

New Year's Reflection, 1991

In 1991, Mike and I heli-skied Adamants, staying at 15,700 feet in the mountain lodge, which was only in its third week of operation. It was five degrees below (Fahrenheit), requiring an extra sweater. Mike got the flu but recovered enough to enjoy some skiing. We talked about how good and important it is to have someone to share special moments with. The only real downside of the trip was not being able to spend New Year's Eve with Fern.

Racing an Avalanche, 1992

I was skiing Revelstoke in 1992 in 18-inch light powder, just floating down the mountain, sailing over rises and sinking back into the soft depressions of snow with seemingly no effort. I felt exaltation with each thrilling turn down the mountain. My newly acquired Miller Softs, wide skis considered the best powder boards at that time, were a supplemental aid to what felt like skimming on top of the white world of snow. It was the perfect ski day, until the world started to slide.

Avalanches in the virgin snow were always a real danger, but that day, they became more real.

My guide and I were stopped at the bottom of a clear run, when I heard a loud "whump!" like dynamite exploding, and the snow began moving under and over my skis. In the suddenness of it all, I was glued in place until someone from behind me yelled, "Get the hell out of here!" Leaden though my body seemed, I streaked sideways until I was out of the slide area.

Safely out of the path of the tumbling banks of snow, I looked upslope to see a fellow in our group named Bob, a big guy, 230 pounds and 6'3" trying to stay on his skis as the avalanche carried him down the hill. He was skiing for his life, as fast as he could, down some 400 yards before the white earth slowed and settled.

Even Bob couldn't believe he was still standing. No one was caught by the avalanche that day, thank God! But what a sight. And what a near disaster.

Pack Man, February 1993

One time, after a glorious morning on Revelstoke in dusty, cold powder 12 to 18 inches deep, the best day by far of that trip, we were on the last run. I was "pack man," carrying the emergency pack, and thus the last down. I was skiing fast, yodeling, enjoying the rush when I glanced to my right and saw the underside of about 12 inches of a ski tip. It wasn't moving. I stopped and yelled, but there was no answer. I stared for another few seconds. Still no motion. My heart panicked. No one else was in sight. I headed over to the ski.

Dave, a member of our group, had tumbled off a slight rise head first into a hole in the hollow snow and just twisted at the last minute so his face and one arm were upward and free, but covered so all that was visible was that one small tip. The snow was packed so firmly around him, he couldn't move his ski.

Luckily, Herb in our group had chanced to look back and saw me rush off to the side. Sensing something was wrong, he climbed back up. Because I had the pack, we had a radio and radioed the group to let them know the situation. It took twenty minutes for both of us to dig him out. Dave never could have gotten out alone. What a save!

I had been a little tempted to ski ahead even when I had the pack in order to experience the untouched snow. No more!

"Now hereafter for sure I'll stay back as rescue pack man when I carry the pack!" I declared in my journal.

My Attitude About Skiing and Life, 1994

In January 1994, I was once again up in the Selkirks heliskiing. Along with the other skiers, I climbed into the helicopter at

1980s

base camp in thick fog, but rising above the mountains we came into sunshine and picture book clouds, the mountains' singular tops quiet and stately below us. It was heavenly. Beautiful. I remembered making a comment like this to Mike one time, and he replied, "Not nearly as beautiful as heaven will be." I felt a wonderful moment of gratitude.

Our helicopter landed at the top of the mountain, and I proceeded to glide silently, softly down on the upper slopes between the trees that had been bent at the top as though humbled by the wind and frosted completely like giant wedding cakes. The crystalline surface of the snow sparkled in varying colors like the finest diamonds in a golden floodlight from the sun. The day was prettier than any I'd ever seen out there in God's wonderful snowy mountains. It was great skiing too.

Stopping to rest I observed one crystal on a mossy branch, overly long, resembling the most intricate lace-like web of hoarfrost, the entire micro scene backlit with the low-lying sunlight and made fairytale-like by the vast rocky peaks in the background.

In a winter wonderland, 1990s

In heliskiing, you always ski as a group for safety, but our group somehow seemed a lot closer to one another that day as we all did very well and bonded as a result. It was an extreme pleasure and satisfaction. The only thing better would have been to share it with relatives and loved ones.

The Beauty and Joy of Heliskiing

This entry from my 1994 journal just about sums up why I loved heliskiing so much.

In Mica Creek village, standing on the same level as the Columbia River, its icy cold water flowing past us, the chopper noisily breezed in to pick up eleven of us to take us to the top of Adamants. It was a most promising day with bright blue skies and a feathery 18 inches of new powder.

As the day progressed, I skied better, and the old legs got into a mode that seemed almost effortless down the very steep, wooded slopes. Silently and smoothly, I made graceful turns that day, so timely and symmetrically in tune with the contours and sometimes sharp drops, I literally flew off the rises and landed on the cotton-soft fluff in a cloud of powder with my heart almost in my mouth and breaths coming in grunts and puffs. No skiing could ever be more pleasurable, gliding across the open glaciers bound only by the bright blue sky above dotted with puffy white clouds and the earth below me, stretching into God's most glorious array of jagged snow-covered peaks and mountain ranges as far as the eye could see in every direction.

As we entered the tree line and dashed between sets of pines like a slalom course, the excitement rose. The grade steepened, and we seemed to plunge as we were dropping. Shorter turns were necessary to contain our pathway and control speed. It became a magnificent contentment to master this game. Not crashing, not jerking, but moving gracefully and beautifully through the giant tree slalom, I went downward, downward until I felt if I didn't stop to rest, I would just become a liquid and melt into the white softness. Wow!!

My panting and puffing were all the sound I could hear, until I let out a gigantic yodel, venting the exhilaration to the others. Fun, fun, fun!

Down the Waterfall, 1994

The next day after I wrote that was a Thursday. On the 3:15 run, the last of the day, I was the first over the edge racing through the trackless powder just behind the guide, Roger. I thought of the rest of my group, empathizing the possible feeling of envy of my ten mates, who must follow a not quite trackless path.

Magical snow! 1984

One run or burst was about three minutes, and then I would stop to rest. Still just behind the guide, the second burst took me through tighter pathways and shallower snow. But then he didn't stop for a while. In the rhythm of the turns, he just kept going, which he wasn't supposed to do. I kept after him as best I could but finally wearied I thought, "I'm going to let him go." I turned out leftward for a rest stop at the edge of an open white, treeless area.

That's when it happened.

The snow caved away under my skis, and I dropped straight down some twelve feet so fast I didn't realize what was happening. My skis hit near vertical snow, tipped, and I slid head downward another 25 feet or so into a freezing cold waterfall coming out of the hill at 90 degrees from my line.

I sunk head first into the water between icy banks (vertical almost) and the side of my head crashed against a rock, sort of blacking me out. I pulled my head up and as I recovered my senses, I looked upward and caught a glimpse of sky. Only for a few seconds though. Just then the deep snow slid in from behind and enwrapped me. All light disappeared and for a few moments, I realized that I might be buried there and never found. Cheap funeral!

The waterfall continued gushing, however, and washed the snow cover away, exposing the wonderful welcome blue of the sky once again. As I lay there, sort of wedged into the falls, I wondered how and if I would be found. The water, probably around 33 degrees, was washing into my suit, filling my boots, and I was afraid to move for fear of falling the remaining 45 feet down the waterfall and disappearing into the large black opening in the snow that was swallowing the falls below and seemed to be beckoning.

I found, assessing my situation, that I had one ski and one pole. The rest of my equipment was gone. I wanted to reach down and release the ski and salvage it but as I moved, my ribcage screamed with pain. I struggled and finally released the ski with the pole and watched it swoosh away into the oblivion with a frightening rush, warning me to move carefully.

I shouted to my fellow skiers. Thankfully, one skied close enough to hear me and warn the others who were below. At least now there might be some way out of this! The water splashed so loudly I could scarcely hear their encouragements but knew they would be my saviors. After determining I wasn't bleeding badly, because my hat and goggles padded the blow, I pulled up on the overhanging ice and stood on one leg, my only solid ground a plate-sized rock in the midst of the vertical falls surrounded by snow. What a sight it must have been from below as I began to grunt, pull, dig, slowly stand and balance, and pray, trying all the while to not look down. All they could see was my head and arms for a while as I yelled for a rope to help pull me up and use as insurance against any further plunge, which would be fatal and final into that black hole.

They had no rope. It was up to me to get out of there.

Scared and shivering, I carefully chopped a notch in the snow and ice to my right with my boot, carving a sort of ledge as flat as I could in the 70-degree angle snow, then I went slowly down to my knees, praying that neither I nor the snow and ice supporting me would suddenly release and plunge all together into that abyss 40 feet below.

The pain in my ribs and the intense chill miraculously left me as the task to carve more ledge took all my concentration. It was slow-going. With each new notch in the snow, each new landing, I slid my knees sideways, a little farther, a little farther, until finally Bill Pence in our group, who had taken off his skis and waited on the snowbank beside the falls, grabbed me and pulled me to safety.

All was anti-climactic after that as the helicopter (then at 4:15 p.m.) found a place to land to pick me up—ski-less—and take me back to the lodge at Mica Creek. Lord, thank you once again!

Back at the lodge, further exam by Bill and later Rick Pence and Dr. Stanley revealed separated rib cartilage, neck whiplash, a pulled muscle at my groin, and a deep gash about an inch and a half by three inches on the right side of my forehead. When I took off the bandage covering it, some of the guys said the gash was shaped like the state of Vermont!

I could only sleep on one side that night but slept surprisingly well, perhaps exhausted by the trauma. After breakfast, I said an early good-bye to all and started home, missing two ferries, and finally arriving in Sand Point, Idaho, cold and hungry. I was greeted by my friend and fellow pilot Eric Kasper at about eight in the evening. He flew me through fog and rain to Albany. It was good to be home!

The next Sunday in church, I counted my blessings and once again thanked my Maker.

With fellow heliskiers. I'm in center, standing, circa 2000

Another Scrape with My Creator, 1995

In 1995, I was once again heliskiing. I had turned 70-years old and happened to have a cold bug. I wasn't feeling my best. I reflected in my journal, "Don't know if it's my 70-year old body or this crummy cold, but I actually got tired out there today. We'll see!"

The next day, we were welcomed by six inches of new snow. I was feeling almost well again and had a super time skiing in the trees. But after lunch, I had another scrape with my Creator.

As I hurried to rejoin the group at the side of a run near the tree line, I hit a bump of ice hidden under the powder and tumbled head first about 50 feet down into a tree well. I turned my head just as I went in so it didn't hit the trunk, but there I was, upside down, feet in the air, my face and whole body under the snow and my limbs pinned to my sides.

It happened so quickly I didn't understand at first that I was trapped. The realization of my situation came on slowly and then all at once. I couldn't move an inch. My face was totally covered. I could breathe, for now, but moving my head didn't help. The thick snow shut out any light. My upside-down position was disorienting. As I assessed that it was impossible to move and uncover myself, all of my senses flashed in intense fright. This might be the end, I thought. It was a dark moment.

But my heliskiing buddies, Brian and Brenda (doctor and sister), as our Good Lord ordained, were looking my way from about 100 yards and saw my skis just showing. As I kept reassessing my situation and praying, I was relieved to hear the sound of digging and their voices saying "Dig here, dig here! Pull here."

They told me afterwards it took about 20 minutes to dig me out. I had no sense of time. Time stood still. Even knowing I was being rescued, fright remained buried with me. Totally immobilized, upside down, and in total darkness in that tree well, I had turned blue before they were finally able to drag me up and out.

Shaken and weak, I had no choice but to get back on my skis. Skiing down was the fastest, really the only way off the mountain. It was a half-hour down to the helicopter, and it was tough at first. But the familiarity of the motion, the skis beneath my feet, the sunlight, and having people near me helped to dissipate some of the residual fear and chill leaving me only tired and relieved on the route down the mountain.

Finally, back at the lodge, dry and warm with Advil, a massage, and a good nap, I felt normal again, whatever that is. And wherever that would lead me.

It was a living nightmare, some of the worst fear of claustrophobia I could imagine. It was like a scene in a nail-biter movie, only in real life. I thought, "How wonderful to be alive!"

The next day, I skied in warm, snowy 32 degrees in the lovely bright outdoors. Surely, I thought, He just isn't ready for me yet!

Hitting Three Million Feet, 1996

In 1996, Mike and I were up in the Selkirk mountains enjoying gorgeous new snow on Galena. We got in our ten runs before returning to the lodge, super, great runs even though the snow was heavier on the lower slopes with a temperature of 32 degrees so that it was just like waltzing in the park with each turn.

One of the traditions with CMH was to keep track of your vertical feet. They celebrated every time someone reached a million with a ceremony and the presentation of a new CMH snowsuit.

Mid-morning the next day, our guides announced I had skied 3 million feet. What a number! At the top of the mountain, smoothed over by the night's snowfall, all the guys held poles in an arch in my honor as I skied under them and lead the way down the gorgeous untracked line of the day. It was a delightful milestone.

William Mikkelson

Upon reaching Three Million Feet of Heli-Skiing with CMH. With thanks for your friendship and support over the years.

Mark Kingsbury

Million-Foot Mike, 1997

In February 1997, Mike and I were once again heliskiing, this time staying at the lodge at Cariboos. By then, we had been heliskiing together for ten years and had a great routine. After a stretch class in our room, breakfast, and the usual safety drill, we helicoptered up at 11:30 a.m. There was gorgeous sun and untracked 12-inch powder. What a wonderful day! Mike and I skied in a dreamscape, amazed at God's beautiful wonderland. In at 5:00 p.m., we ate snacks, hot tubbed, stretched, ate dinner, relaxed and went to bed. Another fun day!

Three days later, I got to witness Mike receive recognition for his millionth foot of heliskiing. He led the group down the mountain this time. We skied figure-8's and our friend Rocco took our picture. It was thrilling! That evening, our leader, Ernst made a presentation of a new ski suit to Mike. My son made a very nice speech and thanked me with a tribute, which was very touching. We all cheered, popped champagne, and celebrated.

The Last Helicopter Ride

I heli-skied for the last time in 2002 at 78 years old. It was time to retire from skiing. I love it. I knew I was going to miss it, but the body just couldn't sustain it anymore.

Looking back on those days, they were some of the most memorable of my life! For all the years after, I could close my eyes and feel the powder beneath my gliding skis, relive the delight of each morning as the first sunlight of the day bathed the mountains and moved across the valley. The moments on those mountaintops were so vivid, I could forever replay the events in my head. And they had a mellowing effect as I moved forward in this life. Long afterwards, those memories reminded me how much I always valued and cherished all the gifts God had given to me to use and appreciate.

What a great ride!

Chapter Ten

Looking Back

HELISKIING WAS MEMORABLE AND AMAZING, but the times spent with my family were always the most cherished moments of my life.

How rewarding it has been to see my children grow and love and create wonderful lives for themselves. Each of them is unique, and their lives have not moved along without struggles. No one's does. But my children have accomplished many things. What a wonderful thing for a father to see!

My Accomplished Children

If I had to choose their greatest achievement, I think it is that they are happy in their family lives. They also seem happy in their public lives, as they present themselves to other people and try to share with other people, to support and boost other people as best they can. They've continually contributed to their kids and to their communities and churches. I'm proud of them for sharing with other people and for being content in their lives.

Mike, Jennifer, Gail, Chris, Bobbie, Christmas 1968
After Bob's funeral, Chris, Bobbie, Mike, Fern, me, Jennifer, Gail, December 2006

My family has provided such joy. My kids call me often. I try to telephone them once a week or thereabouts if I don't hear from them. I think they appreciate that. Adding grandchildren and great grandchildren to the Mikkelson tree just added that much more. It is wonderful to spend time with all of them.

Recognizing My Wonderful Children, Grandchildren and Great Grandchildren

At the time of this writing, I am fortunate to have 13 grandchildren and 19 great grandchildren with more on the way.

FROM BOBBIE AND JOHN CLYDE
Anne Louese Clyde Bemis born November 22, 1965 and married to Ken Bemis.
They have two children.
Emily Helen Clyde MacDonald born February 10, 1969 and married to Christian MacDonald.

FROM CHRIS AND ROB MILLER
Aaron Mikkelson Miller, born September 11, 1977, married to Jennifer Jain.
Douglas Robert Miller, born August 7, 1979
Two children.
Ryan William Miller, born May 18, 1982

FROM GAIL AND PAUL NURMI
Alicia Christine born August 20, 1984 and married to Derrick Pelton.
They have two children.
Eric Paul Nurmi born May 22, 1986 and married to Mafalda.
They have one child.

FROM JENNIFER AND JUSTIN HAROLD

Grant William Harold born May 3, 1983 and married to Brittney Summer Harold.
They have two children.
Jenna Eleanor Harold born June 16, 1985 and married to Peter Wayne Moe.
They have one child.

FROM MIKE AND MELISSA MIKKELSON

Melissa Ashley Mikkelson Downs born April 8, 1981 and married to Matthew French Downs.
They have 4 children.
Adam Whitney Mikkelson born March 21, 1983 and married to Chandler Elizabeth Touart.
They have 3 children.
Rebecca Read Mikkelson Butler born August, 24, 1988 and married to Andrew "Bo" Butler.
They have 2 children.
William David Mikkelson born January 23, 1991 and married to Caitlyn Wrenn.

I love you all!

The Mikkelson Family in Mexico, 2001

The Challenges of Aging: Physical Challenges

I've always been relatively healthy, exercising regularly, but with age comes physical challenges. In 1988, it was back and neck issues. In 1989, a torn hernia, requiring surgery, and prostate infection. I went in on a Thursday, Fern taking good loving care of me, and by Saturday I was playing golf. In 1990, I had skin treatment and surgery on the inside of my cheeks with anesthesia to put me out. That was on a Monday. I walked and nursed it for a couple days, proud of myself for not getting restless and Thursday, I played tennis. The doctor took the stitches out later that day.

When I hurt my back heliskiing and had to lie down for thirty days, that was frustrating. I had terrible back pain and just had to wait for it to get better. From day to day, you could hardly tell I was getting better because I was so fragile. It humbled me.

But then and always, I managed to get back up and keep going. And keep a positive attitude. I think that's important.

> ### *A Leader and Teacher*
>
> From his kids to Bill:
>
> Our father greatly influenced us, as a leader and as a teacher in our lives. He was always inclusive and supportive. To this day the grandchildren can't say enough good things about their Grandpa Bill and the experiences they have shared. He is so proud of each of them. In support, Fern and Bill set aside money for their grandchildren's education. $10,000 annually was given, as long as they wrote a letter to their grandparents sharing their goals and aspirations and their progress in their educations. What a gift! All of the grandchildren received this help. He is the essence of a cool grandpa! And DAD!

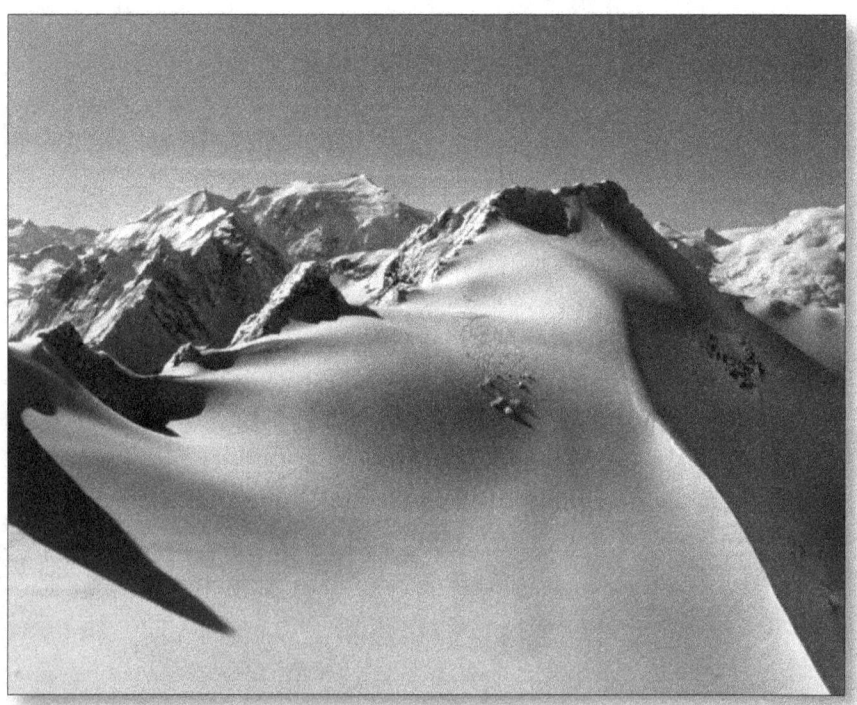

Looking back: At Hoodoo, 1950s
Heliskiing, 1990s

Emotional Challenges: Parents' Passing

Life presents many problems to solve. Sometimes, the emotional part of life can be the most challenging. My father got sick and died in 1980. He was 84 years old, which wasn't bad, but it was sad and strange not to have him around.

My mother continued to be an active part of our lives long after that. Over her lifetime, she contributed a lot to her church and the community. Along with music, she loved raising flowers, reading, and watching sports, particularly basketball.

Towards the end, she was in a wheelchair. That was no burden at all though. There was a nice home in Albany for her when she could no longer live in her house. I never had to be concerned or worried about her, and we'd go visit once in a while. Of course, it became tougher once we moved down to Palm Desert for the winter, and she was up in Albany. She passed away just two months before turning 99 years old in March 1996. Even though we knew it was coming, it was still sad, and we missed her. She really gave Bob and me everything a mother has to give.

(Top) My parents Alice and Harry
(Above) My mother Alice, 1996

A Photo with Alice

From my journals:
> July 1989
>
> Great, gigantic celebration of family! All five youngun's and 11 of 12 grandchildren were on hand. (Emily had returned to Boston to work as a nanny.) What a joy! All arrived about 12:30 and the photographer sort of took over. Sun peeked in and out but finally presented a desired overcast (we had worried about rain). Group pics in backyard with lots of comic relief. Should get some memorable pics. Little ones played badminton, basketball, pool, foosball and generally added controlled pandemonium and all enjoyed a tasty brunch and lots of getting reacquainted. Fern and I are swelling with pride and overwhelmed with the Lord's wonderful gifts. We truly are rich!
>
> Grandma Alice is in her glory, surrounded by all her loved ones. Great memories created this day as we all separated to live individual scenarios and perhaps will not all gather at one place again, at least for a long time. Paul and gang left about 4pm, no clouds but headwinds.
>
> So wonderful to wake up and have the house full of noise and vibrancy!

Looking back: With brother Bob in high school, 1941
Donning the old sweaters again for our 40th high school reunion, 1981

Losing Fern

Fern's passing in March 2013 was one of the hardest experiences I've ever endured. We had a wonderful relationship and life together and 67 years of marriage. I kept thinking after it happened, the way it happened that she didn't have to die, not then.

One night, she awoke to a terrible headache and neck pain. In the morning, I took her to the hospital. They kept her there for three or four hours, until the doctor said, "Well, we've done enough tests." Then they sent us home, but she was still hurting.

That same day, she collapsed with a massive stroke. By ambulance, we rushed back to the hospital, but it was too late.

In hospice care, Fern was lying quietly. I lay on her bed alongside her feeling her warmth. The doctor came in, and I quietly asked him, "Is there any way I might go with her?"

Knowing the answer was in God's hands, he left the room. The nurse returned handing me a poem that he had written to answer my plea. It spoke to just how I was feeling at that time:

> Fern,
> You are my journey
> You are my destination
> I lay beside you, and
> Feel you slip away
>
> What a hindrance my life is…
> As my soul can't keep pace.

It just felt afterwards that I could've done more. If I had that morning to do over again, if we had stayed in the hospital, could something have been done? But that's the way God was meant to have it happen, I guess.

I'm very blessed to have had Fern as my wife, my friend and partner through life. We led a great life together. She was calm and soft-spoken. Sweet. We never shouted at one another. We never had an argument involving a verbal yelling match, never. And she tolerated me being me, off in all these different directions. She flowed with me when I'd tell her I had invited a friend for dinner that night or "we're going dancing" or "we're getting on a plane." We enjoyed each other, raising kids, playing tennis and traveling together.

Looking back: In front of our new house, 1961
Enjoying good times, circa 2001

Before our 67 years of marriage, 1943

She managed five pregnancies, handled everything to do with home and our kids and never seemed to yell at them. It was a lot of work, but she kept everything running and with positivity. She had good friends and helped in the community. She was a great woman.

Just before her funeral, I managed to write this tribute:

My first introduction to beauty was when I met Fern. She was sixteen with brightness glowing all about her.

Driving the family car with her new license, an aura of gorgeous loveliness, long blonde hair, slim, healthy figure and an infectious warming grin.

I was bashful and afraid of pretty girls, but this one welcomed me, banished my shyness as I touched her dainty hands.

This must have been what love was meant to be for me, and we spent 67 years amusing and enjoying each other and growing together as God must have ordained.

I used to say the proposal included a phrase:

"Fern, I bet you're afraid to marry me."

Well, she called my bet and raised me five!

Kind of corny—but a storybook on how to raise kids.

She was an expert, wonder woman, mom, and we all bathed in her tender, caring adoration.

Each morning as she kissed me, she would say, "Go get 'em, Honey! You can do it!"

Words of Wisdom

I'm not sure how wise I am, but I guess I've learned a thing or two over the years. I believe in helping others, loving and appreciating family, faith, being active, trying new things, hard work. I was rewarded for my hard work, I really was. I've benefitted greatly from the teaching of others, especially through my church. So, here's some philosophy that means a lot to me and hopefully is worth passing on to my grandchildren and great grandchildren, and maybe even their children.

Steering Your Life

There are many things we can't control. You can't stop the storm, but you can land the plane, fly it high or fly it low. You have a choice. These are quotes I wrote in one of my journals from a leadership training with my church. I found them inspiring and learned from reflecting on them:

> "There is no meaning to life except the meaning man gives his life by the unfolding of his powers."
> - Erich Fromm

> One ship drives East and the other drives West
> With selfsame winds that blow.
> 'Tis the set of the sails
> And not the gales
> Which tells us the way to go."
> - Ella Wheeler Wilcox, "The Wind of Fate,"
> *The Best-Loved Poems of Americans*, 1976

Decide on Happiness

Be happy. Don't ever be growly. Just be happy. And happiness is composed of what you make it. It's your own possession, and you do it or not. It's an important starting place, because you're much more successful at whatever you do if you're happy doing it.

It may sound simple, but I don't think a lot of people understand that. They look for happiness outside themselves. Happiness doesn't happen outside.

Try New Things

I was always trying new things, and I think that served me well. And when I did, I put effort into the activities. I had the opportunity to write for the town newspaper when I was in high school and learned to write better. Starting married life in Albany, I tried new ventures. I had those stamp machines on posts around town, making a few dollars a week. That business didn't work. A dozen others didn't work either. And each one took time and effort and some dollars. But I never remember being disappointed in any. I learned something from each one and kept trying: crop dusting, freezers and food plans, the corner burger shop, raising turkeys. They all taught me something. There was always a new idea or project! I guess I never thought anything was impossible. I wanted a successful business of my own and that desire drove me to take risks. The mini-storage warehouses and self-service laundries worked out. The Savings and Loan did for a while. Smoke-Craft and the truck stop did as well.

The same was true in ski jumping, heli-skiing and in entering competitions like the senior golf tournament and various tennis tournaments. I had a goal. In order to accomplish that goal, I had to take risks. It was just part of it. And I had to work hard at each thing.

Looking back: With my plane in Tahoe, circa 1972
With my plane in Palm Desert, 2002

As a result, I had many interests along the way. My kids might tease me that as well as "playing hard," I had the philosophy: he who dies with the most toys wins! But they were mostly "toys" that supported my interests: airplanes, a ski boat, good skis, racquets, clubs, that sort of thing. And I was fortunate to have the money to buy them.

Keep Learning

I always tried to grow and learn.

One example was when I attended Presbyterian Family Camp in 1988. I did Intention Training, some counseling and reflection exercises. Some of the notes in my journal from that day reminded me to "Try to believe that I am excellent, that I am fortunate, that I have experience."

I've had many happenings in my life, and there aren't any important happenings that I missed that either can be made up for or must be experienced or made up for. I was reminded that pain and discomfort will pass. Also "if my behavior benefits me, I will continue it." And "Stop accusing others of being wrong…and the door will open."

Having an intent to learn is important and helps you become a better person.

Helping Others & Being Part of a Community

Helping others is just what you do. It makes your life richer.

When I was able to, I backed people financially whose ideas I heralded. I helped family members when hit with financial troubles. I tried to always be there for my kids with hopefully practical advice and help. I stayed involved in my church and community always.

Choosing Relationships

When engaging in any relationship, I have to make sure that it's sincere, that the people involved are not just trying to make me feel good. I try to look at the total situation. If they do something for me or ask me for something, I take time to reflect and observe: What are they doing this for? Why are they asking? I evaluate the answers.

I've always made an effort to keep in touch with friends and was fortunate to have so many over the years, including many lifelong friends.

You Are a Gift

A message I would like to leave with my grandchildren and their children is this: you have to respect yourself first. You are a gift of God. If you can do your best at any one task, I don't care what that task is, you do your best, and you keep talking to yourself and loving yourself. I hope that will have an impression on them.

I have so very much to be thankful for.

And thank you for reading!

Flying High

www.ingramcontent.com/pod-product-compliance
Lightning Source LLC
Chambersburg PA
CBHW050126170426
43197CB00011B/1735